How Serious a Problem Is Synthetic Drug Use?

Other titles in the *In Controversy* series:

How Serious a Problem Is Synthetic Drug Use?

Peggy J. Parks

INCONTROVERSY

ReferencePoint
Press®

San Diego, CA

© 2016 ReferencePoint Press, Inc.
Printed in the United States

For more information, contact:
ReferencePoint Press, Inc.
PO Box 27779
San Diego, CA 92198
www. ReferencePointPress.com

LIBRARY OF CONGRESS CATALOGING-IN-PUBLICATION DATA

Parks, Peggy J., 1951–
  How serious a problem is synthetic drug use?/by Peggy J. Parks.
    pages cm. -- (In controversy)
  Includes bibliographical references and index.
   ISBN 978-1-60152-884-1 (hardback) -- ISBN 1-60152-884-1 (hardback) 1. Drug abuse--United States--Juvenile literature. 2. Synthetic drugs--Juvenile literature. I. Title.
  HV5825.P2853   2016
  362.29'90973--dc23

                                            2015021951

Contents

Foreword

In 2008, as the US economy and economies worldwide were falling into the worst recession since the Great Depression, most Americans had difficulty comprehending the complexity, magnitude, and scope of what was happening. As is often the case with a complex, controversial issue such as this historic global economic recession, looking at the problem as a whole can be overwhelming and often does not lead to understanding. One way to better comprehend such a large issue or event is to break it into smaller parts. The intricacies of global economic recession may be difficult to understand, but one can gain insight by instead beginning with an individual contributing factor, such as the real estate market. When examined through a narrower lens, complex issues become clearer and easier to evaluate.

This is the idea behind ReferencePoint Press's *In Controversy* series. The series examines the complex, controversial issues of the day by breaking them into smaller pieces. Rather than looking at the stem cell research debate as a whole, a title would examine an important aspect of the debate such as *Is Stem Cell Research Necessary?* or *Is Embryonic Stem Cell Research Ethical?* By studying the central issues of the debate individually, researchers gain a more solid and focused understanding of the topic as a whole.

Each book in the series provides a clear, insightful discussion of the issues, integrating facts and a variety of contrasting opinions for a solid, balanced perspective. Personal accounts and direct quotes from academic and professional experts, advocacy groups, politicians, and others enhance the narrative. Sidebars add depth to the discussion by expanding on important ideas and events. For quick reference, a list of key facts concludes every chapter. Source notes, an annotated organizations list, bibliography, and index provide student researchers with additional tools for papers and class discussion.

The *In Controversy* series also challenges students to think critically about issues, to improve their problem-solving skills, and to sharpen their ability to form educated opinions. As President Barack Obama stated in a March 2009 speech, success in the twenty-first century will not be measurable merely by students' ability to "fill in a bubble on a test but whether they possess 21st century skills like problem-solving and critical thinking and entrepreneurship and creativity." Those who possess these skills will have a strong foundation for whatever lies ahead.

No one can know for certain what sort of world awaits today's students. What we can assume, however, is that those who are inquisitive about a wide range of issues; open-minded to divergent views; aware of bias and opinion; and able to reason, reflect, and reconsider will be best prepared for the future. As the international development organization Oxfam notes, "Today's young people will grow up to be the citizens of the future: but what that future holds for them is uncertain. We can be quite confident, however, that they will be faced with decisions about a wide range of issues on which people have differing, contradictory views. If they are to develop as global citizens all young people should have the opportunity to engage with these controversial issues."

In Controversy helps today's students better prepare for tomorrow. An understanding of the complex issues that drive our world and the ability to think critically about them are essential components of contributing, competing, and succeeding in the twenty-first century.

Chasing a Deadly High

On February 7, 2015, Grant Hobson left his home in Lake Conroe, Texas, to spend the night with a friend. His parents were comfortable with his plans; they knew and liked Grant's friend, and they trusted their son. Both teens were honor students and members of their high school debate team, and they were preparing for a prestigious Harvard University debate tournament. The Hobsons had no idea that there was another reason for the get-together: The two boys were taking part in a drugging and texting party. Plans had been made ahead of time for teens at several different homes to take N-Bomb (a powerful synthetic hallucinogen), at the exact same moment. Afterward they would all share their psychedelic experiences through group texting.

Grant never got the chance to talk about his experience with N-Bomb. Shortly after he placed the drug-soaked stamp on his tongue, his vital organs shut down. Although he was rushed to an area hospital, there was nothing doctors could do for him. At the age of sixteen Grant was declared to be brain-dead. A month later his father, Tyler Hobson, spoke publicly about his family's grief over Grant's death. "I was one of those people who really didn't understand the synthetic world," he said, "and am beginning to understand how incredibly horrible it is."[1] Tyler's lack of knowledge about synthetic drugs is disturbingly common. Even though awareness of these substances has grown in recent years, many people still do not know much about them—including how dangerous they can be.

Chemical Calamity

The word *synthetic* means artificial, or manmade, and synthetic drugs are substances that are created (synthesized) from chemical processes. This differentiates the drugs from those made of plant material, such as marijuana (cannabis plant), morphine (opium poppies), and cocaine (coca leaf). Some synthetic drugs, including methamphetamine (crystal meth), MDMA (ecstasy or Molly), and phencyclidine (PCP or angel dust), have existed for decades. But the current, widespread alarm over synthetic drugs refers to a relatively new group of substances whose existence in the United States has been known for less than a decade. To date, the Drug Enforcement Administration (DEA) has identified nearly three hundred synthetic drugs that are loosely categorized into three groups: cannabinoids, cathinones, and what the DEA refers to as "powerful hallucinogenic compounds."[2]

N-bomb, the drug that killed Grant Hobson, is part of the last group along with a number of other synthetic hallucinogens. These are powerful synthetic drugs that are said to mimic the hallucinogenic effects of LSD at a much cheaper price—but they have proved to be dangerous and unpredictable. "The potential for experiencing significant toxicity seems to be extremely high for this drug," says Joji Suzuki, director of the division of addiction psychiatry at Brigham and Women's Hospital in Boston, Massachusetts. "I don't think this is the most toxic drug out there, but there's a deceptive piece to it. Many of the kids who got sick had experience with LSD. So it gives a false sense of security."[3]

Synthetic cannabinoids are designed to mimic delta-9-tetrahydrocannabinol (THC), the psychoactive ingredient in marijuana. The chemicals are sprayed onto dried, shredded plant material that is sold under a wide variety of names, including Spice, K2, Black Mamba, Kush, and Scooby Snax. Because the drugs physically resemble marijuana and are smoked, they are often called synthetic marijuana or "fake pot"—but this comparison is misleading. Experts say synthetic cannabinoids can be fifty to one hundred times more potent than marijuana.

Synthetic cathinones are stimulant drugs that are so named

Synthetic cannabinoids—sold under various names, including Spice—are designed to mimic THC, the psychoactive ingredient in marijuana. The resemblance ends there; synthetic cannabinoids are far more potent than marijuana.

because they stimulate the central nervous system. These are chemical versions of cathinone, an organic substance that comes from the plant *Catha edulis* (khat), which is grown in East Africa and the Arabian Peninsula. Synthetic cathinones are sold under a variety of names such as Purple Wave, Blue Silk, White Dove, Bliss, Vanilla Sky, and Ocean Burst. The newest member of the synthetic cathinone family is alpha-PVP, more commonly known as *flakka* or by its street name, *gravel*. Since flakka first emerged in South Florida during late summer 2014, abuse of the drug has soared, with numerous cases of bizarre, psychotic behavior exhibited by those who have taken it. Health officials consider flakka to be one of the most threatening synthetic drugs, and the National Institute on Drug Abuse (NIDA) refers to it as a "dangerous synthetic cathinone."[4]

One of the most frightening aspects of synthetic drugs is that users are taking them without knowing who made them, where they were made (most often China), and what is in them—so they have no idea what chemicals they are ingesting. "Using these synthetic drugs is like doing a chemistry experiment in your body," says Mike Barbour, a chief nursing officer at a Panama City, Florida, hospital. "You have no idea what the outcome is going to be."[5] To skirt drug laws and to give their products a less harmful appearance, drug makers resort to unscrupulous tactics. Synthetic cannabinoids, for instance, are often marketed as herbal incense or potpourri. Synthetic cathinones are sold as bath salts, even though they have nothing to do with bathing. To further the deception both types of drugs are deceptively labeled "Not for human consumption." Should the drugs be confiscated by law enforcement and banned under state or federal law, manufacturers simply tweak the chemical formulas slightly so they are technically no longer illegal.

Widespread Abuse

Because of all the mysteries surrounding synthetic drugs, no one knows exactly how many types exist or how many people use them. Agencies such as the DEA and NIDA closely monitor drug trends and strive to keep the public informed. In addition, the American Association of Poison Control Centers (AAPCC) maintains the only near real-time comprehensive poisoning surveillance database in the United States. The AAPCC reports that between January 1, 2015, and April 22, 2015, there was a dramatic spike in calls to American poison centers about adverse reactions to new synthetic cannabinoids. In less than three months, nineteen hundred emergency calls were received—fifteen hundred in April alone. This was nearly four times the number of synthetic drug-related poison center calls during the same period in 2014. "This is the worst outbreak of drug abuse that I've lived through," says Steven Marcus, executive director of the New Jersey Poison Information and Education System at Rutgers University. "It's almost as if someone had made a witches' brew of these cannabinoids."[6]

The resurgence of poison center calls was particularly alarming because it occurred after a steady downward trend in such calls. According to a February 2015 DEA report, after a peak of 6,968 calls in 2011, by 2013 the number had sharply dropped to 2,639. Yet health officials emphasize that the decline does not necessarily indicate a decline in synthetic drug abuse. "Experts agree that the number of calls to poison control centers initially skyrocketed because of the unfamiliarity with the drugs and how to counter their effects," says the DEA. "As [emergency room] doctors have become aware of how to treat victims of synthetic cannabinoid and cathinone abuse, the number of calls to poison control centers has naturally declined."[7]

A "New Frontier"

Health officials, substance abuse experts, and law enforcement find synthetic drugs to be a formidable problem. The drugs are powerful, unpredictable, and potentially deadly, and after trending downward for several years, prevalence again appears to be on the rise. DEA spokesman Rusty Payne refers to these substances as a "new frontier" for drugs and drug traffickers, and he cautions people about how dangerous they are. "I want to shout it from the roof tops," says Payne. "This is nasty stuff."[8]

Facts

- A study published in April 2013 by Metropolitan Life Foundation and Partnership at Drugfree.org found that 12 percent of teens had used synthetic marijuana (K2 or Spice) during the past year.

- An October 2014 Substance Abuse and Mental Health Services Administration (SAMHSA) report shows that of nearly twenty-three thousand emergency room visits in 2011 involving synthetic drugs, 81 percent were teens or young adults.

- A 2014 NIDA-sponsored survey found that Spice (synthetic cannabinoid) was the second most commonly abused drug among high school seniors after marijuana.

What Are the Origins of the Synthetic Drug Problem?

Prior to the summer of 2010 Mark Ryan had never heard of a synthetic drug called *bath salts*. As director of the Louisiana Poison Center, which is located in the city of Shreveport, Louisiana, Ryan was familiar with most every substance that people took to get high; but not this one. When he got the first phone call about bath salts, his immediate thought was the scented Calgon bath crystals he had seen advertised on TV. "I wondered, people aren't snorting Calgon are they?" says Ryan. "But of course I knew that wasn't it; something else was definitely going on." As it turns out, that "something else" was a synthetic drug crisis that happened fast and hit hard, and it was unlike anything Ryan or his colleagues had ever seen before. "It came on us like a freight train,"[9] he says.

A Crisis Unfolds

Louisiana could easily be called Ground Zero for the onset of the bath salts epidemic. It was one of the first states to discover that people were using these new drugs. This was largely because raw ingredients were being shipped to the Port of New Orleans, Louisiana, from China and other Asian countries and then packaged and sold under the deceptive name *bath salts*. The first call to Ryan's poison center came in September 2010. It was from an emergency room doctor who was very concerned about a distraught patient who had taken the so-called bath salts. The doctor had never seen anyone behave like this, and he wondered if Ryan knew anything about the drug. Ryan did not—but that was about to change.

In October 2010 the Louisiana Poison Center received four calls about bath salts–related emergencies, and a month later the number jumped to twenty-four. By the time December arrived calls to the poison center were coming in regularly, with the number increasing by the day. Ryan had no doubt that he had a major problem on his hands, and he had a strong feeling it was going to get worse.

What struck Ryan as particularly odd was what he was being told by the medical personnel who called him. It was the same story each time: The people who had used bath salts were exhibiting bizarre symptoms such as extreme agitation, confusion, increased heart rate, chest pain, and extraordinarily strange behavior including vivid hallucinations and paranoia. "It was completely off the wall," says Ryan. "All I could think after hearing about the effects of bath salts was a bunch of really bad drugs all lumped together: crazy hallucinations like LSD, out-of-body experiences like PCP, and being super-wired and agitated like cocaine and amphetamines." Another peculiar characteristic shared by bath salts users who experienced hallucinations was their eerily similar descriptions of what they saw. "These guys were seeing monsters, demons, aliens, soldiers pointing guns at them," says Ryan. "We didn't ask, 'Did you see monsters, demons, aliens, and soldiers holding guns?' That's what they said they saw—they told us that."[10]

"All I could think after hearing about the effects of bath salts was a bunch of really bad drugs all lumped together."[10]

— Mark Ryan, director of the Louisiana Poison Center.

Making Sense of a Mystery

Ryan was determined to find out as much as he could about bath salts. He expected his colleagues in major metropolitan areas like New York City to know about the drugs, but after making some phone calls he soon found that they were as baffled as he was. "At this point I felt like the Lone Ranger,"[11] he says. So he started do-

Louisiana was one of the first states to identify bath salts (pictured) as a dangerous and unregulated drug. Poison control officials in that state began receiving calls about bath salts–related emergencies in 2010.

ing his own research, collecting packages of bath salts from the police, from emergency room personnel, and from stores that carried it—including online marketplaces like Amazon.com. Ryan found an out-of-state laboratory that could test the substances and sent the bath salts to them to find out what chemicals they contained. He learned that these were compounds known as synthetic cathinones, which had originally been created for research but were being used to manufacture bath salts.

Ryan then collaborated with Henry A. Spiller, director of the Kentucky Poison Center, because he was also dealing with an influx of calls about bath salts. To create an extensive database Ryan began collecting case reports and product samples from both centers.

Collectively, the two poison centers had reports of 236 patients who were seen for emergency care, with most of them youth and 78 percent male. Among the patients, all had used synthetic cathinones, of which 37 different brand names were identified. "Out of that collaboration," says Ryan, "came a paper which to date is the largest series of case reports about synthetic cathinones."[12] The paper, which was published in the scientific journal *Clinical Toxicology*, was titled "Clinical Experience with and Analytical Confirmation of 'Bath Salts' and 'Legal Highs' (Synthetic Cathinones) in the United States."

Taking Action

In early December 2010 the Louisiana Poison Center was inundated with calls about bath salts emergencies, and there was no sign of a slowdown. So Ryan sent out a bulletin to other poison centers throughout the United States to warn them of what was going on: "I told them, you may not have heard of this bath salts drug yet, but trust me, you will."[13] On Christmas Eve Ryan's home phone was ringing off the hook with calls for the poison center. He and his family were packed and ready to fly to Colorado for a skiing vacation, when he realized there was no possible way he could leave. The situation was dire and growing worse by the minute, and he needed to see it through.

On Christmas Day, which is typically a slow time for the poison center, emergency calls started early in the morning and were coming in fast, one after another. By the time Ryan had taken the eleventh call, he knew that he had made the right decision by staying home—and he also knew that he was facing a major public health crisis. So he telephoned Jimmy Guidry, Louisiana's state health officer. "Merry Christmas, Jimmy," Ryan said. "I wanted you to know that my family has gone skiing and I'm staying here. We've got a crisis on our hands and I'm afraid it's going to require some drastic measures."[14]

After talking with Ryan, Guidry was ready to do whatever needed to be done. It was a sticky situation, though, because unlike illicit drugs such as heroin, marijuana, or cocaine, bath salts were not illegal. They were manufactured from legal substances

A Cannabinoid Pioneer

In the early 1960s Israeli scientist Raphael Mechoulam became the first to identify and synthesize the psychoactive ingredient in marijuana known as THC. During animal studies he spent years researching cannabinoid receptors, which are specific proteins within brain and spinal cord cells that bind to THC when someone smokes marijuana. Mechoulam coined the term *cannabinoids* after the cannabis plant, and referred to his research as "cannabinoid chemistry."

In 1992 Mechoulam discovered a cannabinoid that exists naturally in the brain. Likening it to the body's own natural THC, he and his colleagues named it *anandamide*, taken from the Sanskrit term for eternal bliss or supreme joy. Two years later researchers identified another natural cannabinoid and named it 2-AG. "By using a plant [cannabis] that has been around for thousands of years," says Mechoulam, "we discovered a new physiological system of immense importance. We wouldn't have been able to get there if we had not looked at the plant."

Quoted in Martin A. Lee, "The Discovery of the Endocannabinoid System," The Prop 215 Era, July 2012. www.beyondthc.com.

and sold legally in containers marked "Not for human consumption." Says Guidry: "I remember trying to figure out how to approach this. I believed [Ryan] and valued his professional opinion, and I knew we had to do something very serious with the backing of law enforcement."[15]

Guidry put his legal team to work on the project, spent time conferring with law enforcement officials, and carefully evaluated all the data. He determined that bath salts qualified as a dangerous substance that could be banned under state law. His next step was to talk with Ryan about which compounds should be added to the banned list. Ryan gave his recommendation: four that testing had detected in bath salts, and another that was listed on the Internet as a likely ingredient for making the drug. On January 6, 2011, Guidry used a state measure called an emergency rule to ban five synthetic cathinones used in the manufacture of bath salts. Based on this ruling, the powerful stimulants methylenedioxypyrovalerone (MDPV) and mephedrone, as well as methylone, methedrone, and flephedrone, became illegal under Louisiana law. Ryan says that upon hearing about the bans in Louisiana, Florida officials banned the exact same substances. One by one, other states began to follow their lead.

Influx of "Incense"

The bath salts crisis in 2010 and 2011 was the first known appearance of synthetic cathinones in the United States, but it was not the first incident involving synthetic drugs. Synthetic cannabinoids had been discovered by officials from the US Customs and Border Protection (CBP) several years before that—although the drug manufacturers went out of their way to conceal the true identity of their products.

In late 2007 inspectors from the CBP in Wilmington, Ohio, began noticing a steady stream of packages marked *herbal incense*. At the time, Wilmington was a major distribution hub for the worldwide shipping company DHL, and these particular shipments were coming in on a regular basis. Knowing this was out of the ordinary, the inspectors opened the boxes and found that the contents were all exactly the same. Each box held about a dozen small, shiny foil packets that contained an herbal mixture marked with the brand name Spice. The officers wondered what possible reason anyone could have for paying to express-ship cartons and cartons of herbal incense to the United States. As peculiar as the shipments seemed to be, however, testing consistently showed that the foil packets contained no illegal substances. Thus, the CBP officers had no grounds to keep them from being released into US commerce.

Like his colleagues, CBP agricultural specialist Steven Bishop became intrigued with the ongoing arrivals of herbal incense, especially because the number of shipments was growing. So Bishop,

Louisiana's state health officer Jimmy Guidry and his legal team determined that bath salts qualified as a dangerous substance. The next step was to find a way to ban the substance under state laws.

who is a botanist, began to analyze the herbs that were listed on the packet labels. He also conducted some online research and made an interesting discovery. People in parts of Europe were smoking the so-called incense and, as Bishop explains, were claiming to have had "massive, massive highs from this product."[16] He had doubts about the claim since he knew that the herbs he had identified could not have caused such an effect.

Bishop strongly suspected that there was something far more potent than herbs in the packets, and as he continued his research he grew even more certain of that. He read about a powerful synthetic cannabinoid called HU-210, which had been developed for brain research by Israeli scientists in the late 1980s. Bishop learned that the substance produced many of the same effects as the natural THC found in marijuana but was far stronger and more potent than THC. Also, once someone used the synthetic drug, its effects lasted much longer than the effects of marijuana. The more Bishop thought about it, the more certain he was that the packages of "herbal incense" contained HU-210. Yet at that point it was still only a suspicion.

Busted

In November 2008 several large shipments from the Czech Republic came through the DHL port in Wilmington. Like previous shipments these were filled with shiny foil packets of Spice, but there were fifteen hundred packets in each container. Bishop immediately sent samples to the CBP testing laboratory in Chicago, Illinois, which had conducted previous testing on the packages of herbs. This time Bishop specifically asked chemist Bill Wagner to test for traces of HU-210, which had not been done before. The testing was difficult, tedious, and took a very long time—but it proved to be fruitful. After more than ten hours of analyzing one packet of Spice, Wagner discovered that it contained HU-210 along with two other synthetic cannabinoids. What he found was disturbing to him. "These packets were lethal," says Wagner. "There were three synthetics in the mix and it was a deadly combination. I can't imagine anybody not having bad effects after smoking that mess."[17]

Based on Wagner's discovery the shipments at the Wilmington DHL facility were seized by CBP officials. As a result, says a CBP publication, "the lid was irreparably blown off of the murky world of the designer drug trade."[18] Wagner contacted the DEA to explain what the CBP lab had uncovered. The following March an intelligence alert about the lab's discovery was included in the DEA's law enforcement newsletter *Microgram Bulletin*. Although the DEA had been aware of the existence of synthetic drugs, Wagner's lab analysis was the first tangible evidence of it.

"There were three synthetics in the mix and it was a deadly combination. I can't imagine anybody not having bad effects after smoking that mess."[17]

— Bill Wagner, a chemist at the Customs and Border Protection laboratory in Chicago, Illinois.

A Prophetic Scientist

In a 1988 paper, Gary L. Henderson made a prediction about drug abuse in the future. A researcher with the UC Davis School of Medicine's Department of Medical Pharmacology and Toxicology, Henderson had observed abundant, detailed information in scientific literature about how a wide variety of synthetic compounds was created. In his paper he noted that this information could easily be exploited by "clandestine chemists," that restricting access to the publications was not feasible, and that efforts to control the chemicals needed to make synthetic drugs would likely only have minor effects. Henderson wrote: "It is likely that the future drugs of abuse will be synthetics rather than plant products. They will be synthesized from readily available chemicals, may be derivatives of pharmaceuticals, will be very potent, and often very selective in their action. In addition, they will be marketed very cleverly."

There was no way for Henderson to be absolutely certain that his prediction would come true. But today, with the growing problem of synthetic drug use, it is obvious that his words were eerily prophetic.

Gary L. Henderson, "Designer Drugs: Past History and Future Prospects," *Journal of Forensic Sciences*, March 1988, p. 33.

The Hijacking of Medical Research

As profound as the drug bust was, neither the DEA nor the CBP had any idea that their battle with synthetic cannabinoids had barely begun. No one knew at the time that chemical formulas developed for legitimate medical research had been plucked out of scientific journals and exploited by rogue chemists who wanted to profit from them.

The scientist who created these formulas was John W. Huffman, an organic chemist who is widely known for groundbreaking cannabinoid research. Starting in the early 1980s Huffman and his student assistants from Clemson University were studying the interactions between synthetic cannabinoids and cannabinoid receptors in the brain. These receptors are proteins within cells that recognize brain chemicals known as neurotransmitters, and they collectively facilitate the transmission of messages to and from neurons (nerve cells). NIDA explains: "A neurotransmitter and its receptor operate like a 'key and lock,' an exquisitely specific mechanism that ensures that each receptor will forward the appropriate message only after interacting with the right kind of neurotransmitter."[19]

Prior to Huffman's brain studies, researchers from Israel had discovered that when someone uses marijuana, THC binds to cannabinoid receptors. But scientists soon learned that these receptors have functions that go far beyond making someone feel high. "Cannabinoid receptors evolved in all mammalian species and in humans to affect nausea, mood, pain, and inflammation," says Huffman. "They did not evolve so that humans can smoke pot for pleasure."[20] Creating synthetic cannabinoids allowed Huffman to explore the manner in which synthetic compounds interacted with the same receptors as natural THC. He believed that the knowledge gained from this research would be invaluable in developing new medical therapies for a variety of human diseases and disorders.

Huffman and his colleagues spent more than twenty years creating hundreds of synthetic cannabinoids. Most of these were designated by the letters "JWH" (for John W. Huffman) followed by numbers, such as JWH-018 and JWH-073. In 1998 the chemical formula for JWH-018 was included in an article published in the *Journal of Pharmacology and Experimental Therapeutics*. About seven years later a longer, more involved paper about Huffman's JWH-018 research appeared in an article in the *Journal of Bioorganic and Medicinal Chemistry*.

In December 2008 Huffman received an e-mail from a blogger in Germany who had some disturbing news. "One of our compounds, JWH-018, had been identified in a sample of synthetic marijuana sold as 'Spice,'"[21] says Huffman. He learned that a detailed description of the drug had been featured in an arti-

cle published in the German news publication *Der Spiegel* (*The Mirror*). The article explained that people were buying Spice and smoking it to get high.

Huffman and his student assistants had created the compounds strictly for research purposes, but they had no way of stopping rogue chemists from using the formulas to create and sell synthetic drugs. "There are always individuals who will put personal profit ahead of public safety," says Huffman, who goes on to explain:

> Initially it was assumed by many, both in and out of the scientific world, that synthetic cannabinoids are basically just like marijuana. It was soon recognized that they have profoundly different biological effects in humans and were actually very dangerous for human consumption. The compounds are for the most part made in China where no one, probably including the government, cares about toxicity in products for export. . . . I don't believe that most of the small business owners who sell these products realize how dangerous they are.[22]

Federal customs inspectors noticed a steady stream of packages marked "herbal incense" coming through the DHL hub in Ohio beginning in 2007. Testing later showed the contents of the packages, when ingested, could be deadly.

The Real Purpose of Synthetic Cathinones

Richard A. Glennon is another chemist whose scientific formulas were hijacked for purposes very different from what he had intended. During the 1970s and early 1980s Glennon and his colleagues were conducting experiments with laboratory rats. The goal of this research was to determine how various stimulants affected the creatures' brain activity. One experiment involved modifying the stimulant amphetamine to change its molecular structure. In the process, Glennon created beta-keto amphetamine, a substance that later came to be known as methcathinone, or synthetic cathinone. "We didn't expect any type of activity from it," says Glennon, "but we found out it was an active stimulant. And it was at least as potent, if not more potent, than amphetamine."[23]

In 1987 Glennon's findings were revealed in an article titled "Methcathinone: A New and Potent Amphetamine-Like Agent," which was published in the scientific journal *Pharmacology, Biochemistry & Behavior*. The article describes the research conducted by Glennon and his colleagues, and explains how powerful and potent synthetic cathinone is. Not long after the article appeared in print, Glennon was contacted by a scientist from St. Petersburg, Russia. The scientist explained that the same drug that had been called methcathinone had existed for quite a while in the Soviet Union. Investigative journalist Jenny Marder writes: "Methcathinone had sprung up as a major drug of abuse there in the 1970s and had increased tenfold in the eighties. There [in the Soviet Union] they were calling it ephedrone, or 'Jeff' on the streets."[24]

Glennon continued his research and published several dozen papers on synthetic cathinone, including how it affects the brain and how it compares with other substances. For decades, he says, synthetic cathinones were not much of a problem in the United States; rather, they were "more like a theoretical, scientific problem."[25] That changed, however, in 2010 when bath salts started creating havoc in Louisiana—and within a year the problem had spread to every state in the country.

"I don't believe that most of the small business owners who sell these products realize how dangerous they are."[22]

— John W. Huffman, the organic chemist who created synthetic cannabinoids.

The Frightening Unknown

In the years since synthetic cathinones and cannabinoids were first discovered in the United States, these drugs have proved to be powerful, unpredictable, and potentially deadly. Huffman and Glennon, creators of the original chemical formulas, are the first to say that anyone who takes the drugs is flirting with danger. The compounds were meant for research only—not for human use. "To me, one of the most frightening things is that people are experimenting on themselves," says Marilyn Huestis, NIDA's chief of chemistry and drug metabolism. "With most of these designer drugs, we don't even have basic information. We don't know what they do to animals. We don't know what they do to humans. We don't know how toxic they are. And here, you have people taking these drugs."[26]

Although a great deal has been learned about synthetic drugs since Huestis made that statement in 2013, scientists still acknowledge that much remains unknown. That means most users of synthetic drugs have no idea what chemicals they are putting in their bodies or where those chemicals came from.

> "To me, one of the most frightening things is that people are experimenting on themselves."[26]
>
> — Marilyn Huestis, NIDA's chief of chemistry and drug metabolism.

Facts

- The first synthetic cathinone was produced by Russian scientists in 1928 and used as an antidepressant without government officials being aware of it.

- The first person to describe the synthetic stimulant mephedrone was pharmacologist Saem de Burnaga Sanchez, who discussed it in a 1929 scientific journal article.

- Synthetic hallucinogens of the class known as 2C were first synthesized in the 1970s and 1980s by medicinal chemist Alexander Shulgin.

Why Are Young People Drawn to Synthetic Drugs?

Since 2008, when Customs and Border Protection officials first intercepted shipments of Spice entering the United States, the variety of synthetic drugs has grown dramatically. The DEA has identified nearly three hundred of these drugs, including synthetic cannabinoids, synthetic cathinones, and synthetic hallucinogens. People of all ages, from preteens to senior citizens, use synthetic drugs. But based on national surveys, data from poison control centers, and reports from health care providers, it has become evident that the majority of users are younger people. "These substances are marketed to teens and young adults," says Donna M. Lisi, a board-certified psychiatric pharmacist and drug information specialist from New Jersey. "They appeal to young people because they're relatively inexpensive, easily available and aren't detectable on routine drug screens. There's also a major misconception that these drugs are natural, legal, safe and produce less adverse effects than marijuana."[27]

"There's . . . a major misconception that these drugs are natural, legal, safe and produce less adverse effects than marijuana."[27]

— Donna M. Lisi, a board-certified psychiatric pharmacist and drug information specialist from New Jersey.

Deceptive Marketing

One of the main reasons for the misconceptions about synthetic drugs is the way the drugs are packaged and marketed—with young people as the primary target. Medical professionals and those in law enforcement say this is why packages of synthetic cannabinoids come in bright, eye-catching colors, embellished with pictures of clowns or other cartoon characters such as Scooby Doo. These are sales tactics that make the packages appealing to a young audience. "Who doesn't like Scooby Doo," says a Washington, DC, teen who did not want to give his name. "I mean come on."[28]

To further make them seem harmless and fun, synthetic cannabinoids are given playful-sounding names such as Scooby Snax, Angry Birds, Maui Wowie, Crazy Clown, Bling Bling Monkey, Spongebud, and numerous others. The drugs are also offered in a variety of tempting flavors such as cherry, blueberry, grape, mango, strawberry, lemon-lime, watermelon, and bubblegum, which increases their appeal to young people. "Their names may sound harmless and even juvenile," says Raychelle Cassada Lohmann, a licensed therapist and school counselor from South Carolina, "but rest assured they are deadly toxins. With a disclaimer label, 'not for human consumption,' synthetic drugs often disguise the real intent of their use."[29]

In 2015 two girls from Houston, Texas, had no problem buying a brand of synthetic cannabis called "Kush." They purchased the drug, which came in a bright-blue package, at a convenience store. After smoking it the younger of the two, a twelve-year-old middle school student, had a severe reaction to the drug. She lost consciousness and was rushed to the hospital where emergency room doctors and nurses immediately knew what they were facing. They had seen the same symptoms many times before in other young people who took synthetic drugs. The girl was in crisis. Her body temperature had dropped to dangerously low levels, and when a light was shone into her eyes, her pupils did not respond. Yet as serious as her condition was, the girl survived the frightening ordeal and was sent home.

"Their names may sound harmless and even juvenile, but rest assured they are deadly toxins."[29]

— Raychelle Cassada Lohmann, a licensed therapist and school counselor from South Carolina.

Her sister suffered no ill effects from the drug, which health officials say is typical of synthetic drugs—they make one person high, while someone else has a life-threatening reaction.

Caught in the Act

Austin, another major city in Texas, has had a difficult struggle with synthetic drug problems. During 2014, law enforcement and health care providers in Austin began to observe the rapid growth of synthetic cannabinoid abuse, especially among youth. In one month alone more than forty people had serious adverse reactions to the drugs, which led to emergency treatment at area hospitals. To investigate the situation and find out how easy it was for young people to buy the drugs, Austin television station KXAN sent a news reporter to several smoke shops with a hidden camera. Upon entering one of the shops, the reporter noticed a display of colorful, foil-wrapped packages, all of which were labeled *herbal incense* and *not for human consumption*. He showed interest in the products and attracted the attention of a store clerk.

The reporter asked the clerk about the purpose of the products on display. The man explained that the herbal incense was to be put in a warming dish and the scent would fill the room. When questioned about a different package, the clerk said it was a stronger-smelling type of herbal incense. The DEA's Greg Thrash, who was interviewed as part of the news investigation, says he has seen this deceptive method of marketing time after time. What he finds especially frustrating is knowing that young people fall for it just as synthetic drug distributors hope they will. "It's in that pretty package so it's gotta be safe," says Thrash. "That's why a lot of kids get involved with this stuff. Most of them are marketed as incense; believe me, it has nothing to do with incense."[30]

John Bedolla is an emergency medicine physician in Austin who is familiar with synthetic drugs. He has seen their effects for himself because he has treated numerous patients who have been harmed by the drugs. Like Thrash, Bedolla gets extremely frustrated at the deceptive practices used by drug manufacturers, distributors, and sellers. Often, his patients bought synthetic cannabinoids that were labeled *synthetic marijuana* on the package.

"It's basically an advertising ploy," says Bedolla. "They sell you this junk by saying it is like marijuana."[31] He adds that synthetic cannabinoids may be hundreds of times the strength of marijuana and that teens are likely not aware of that when they buy the drug and smoke it.

Seized packages of synthetic cannabinoids are displayed. Playful names and tempting flavors are intended to appeal to young people.

Unknown Dangers

The lack of awareness among young people means they are taking synthetic drugs without knowing what they are or where they came from. "What's scary," says Lohmann, "is teens don't know what they are ingesting when they mess with these toxic substances and neither do the experts." Lohmann denounces anyone who would target young people with products that are dangerous and unpredictable just for the sake of making a profit. "Designer drugs are often manufactured in some underground unsterile laboratory overseas or in someone's basement just down the street," she says. "So who are the experimental guinea pigs? Why our teens of course. In the designer drug industry it's not about the welfare of our youth, or the quality and research behind the product, rather it's all about the money. And this multibillion-dollar industry is booming with success."[32]

The haphazard, imprecise way that synthetic cannabinoids are made is the main reason they are so unpredictable and risky. According to DEA officials, distributors have been found concocting drugs in garages, rented storage units, and even areas where ani-

E-Spice

In recent years electronic cigarettes (e-cigarettes) have soared in popularity. The practice of using e-cigarettes is sometimes called "vaping" because liquid nicotine is converted into an aerosol mist (or vapor) that the user inhales. According to the Centers for Disease Control and Prevention, vaping is soaring in popularity among teens. Between 2013 and 2014 the number of high school students using e-cigarettes jumped from 4.5 percent to 13.4 percent.

The practice of vaping among teens is alarming to health officials for many reasons, especially one that has recently been discovered: Young people are filling the vapor pens with liquid synthetic cannabis and getting high on the vapor. A DEA agent from Denver, Colorado, says this has become the latest trend to attract young people. "It's the cool factor for kids," she says. Denver was the first city to report the practice, and the DEA is trying to get the word out to parents so they can talk to their children about it. But there are challenges. When someone is smoking an e-cigarette, it is virtually impossible to know what he or she is inhaling. "You see a guy using an e-cigarette on a ski lift, at the airport waiting to get on the train, waiting on the corner," says the Denver agent, "You don't know if he's using tobacco, marijuana, or spice."

Quoted in CBS Denver, "New Trend Targets Kids: E-Cigarettes Filled with Spice," May 8, 2014. http://denver.cbslocal.com.

mals are fed. "Basically, they lay this stuff out on a piece of plastic and take something similar to a bug sprayer and just spray it with [...] chemicals," says David Barnes, a sheriff's department captain in Clay County, Florida. Barnes goes on to explain that the difference between one package of synthetic cannabinoids and another hanging on the same store rack can mean the difference between life and death. "There is no consistency of how much of the chemical gets on what part of the product laid out there," says Barnes. "You hypothetically could use the same brand today and smoke it and get high. And use the same brand tomorrow, smoke it and it could be fatal."[33]

This unpredictability applies to all synthetic drugs, not just cannabinoids. When Mark Ryan was developing his database of synthetic cathinone cases in late 2010, he was both disturbed and astonished at the vast difference from one package to another. "We've pulled packages off pegboards in convenience stores," says Ryan, "and from the first to the 20th package, they can be completely different substances. We tested packages of cathinones and found massive discrepancies from one to another."[34]

Ryan emphasizes that the difference between containers of cathinones is profound: One may be 16 milligrams in strength, while another next to it on a shelf or a pegboard could be 2,500 milligrams in strength. "So you have two guys who bought what they thought was the same stuff, at the same time, and they both snorted it," says Ryan. "The drugs get into their systems and one guy starts acting goofy—and the other guy is so out of his mind that doctors have to give him anesthesia to keep him from tearing the emergency room apart." He continues with a stern warning for anyone considering using synthetic drugs: "You do not know what you're taking when you use this stuff. And what that means is you do not know if you're going to live or die after using it."[35]

One sign that teenagers are not fully aware of dangers associated with synthetic drugs is their responses during a national survey known as Monitoring the Future. Sponsored by NIDA, the survey is conducted each year to keep a close watch on substance abuse trends among teenagers in the United States. More than forty-one thousand

"You do not know what you're taking when you use this stuff. And what that means is you do not know if you're going to live or die after using it."[35]

— Mark Ryan, director of the Louisiana Poison Center.

eighth, tenth, and twelfth graders were involved in the 2014 survey, which was published in February 2015. One question asked of students in all three grades was whether they associated great risk with trying synthetic cannabis once or twice. The teens' responses were troubling to health officials: Less than 24 percent of eighth graders thought it was risky to use synthetic cannabis once or twice, and only slightly more tenth graders felt that way. Among seniors, about one-third perceived synthetic cannabis as a risk. The reason these responses were alarming is that if teens do not think synthetic drugs are risky, they are much more likely to use the drugs—and in the process, they are putting their health at risk. The authors of the final report write: "Likely the availability of these drugs over the counter has had the effect of communicating to teens that they must be safe, though they are not."[36]

Soldiers in Mexico prepare to confiscate lab equipment used for making synthetic drugs. These drugs are often made in nonsterile conditions.

Unanswered Questions

When teens have abused synthetic drugs (or any drugs for that matter), it is not unusual for parents to question why they would do such a thing. They wonder what the teens were thinking—or whether they were thinking at all. Did they not know better? Jeanine Motsay was haunted by questions when her sixteen-year-old son, Sam, died after taking N-Bomb. Sam was a sophomore in high school, had a 4.0 grade point average, and had already decided that he was going to study finance in college. He played saxophone with the band and was a forward on his school's junior varsity basketball team. He was a musician, an athlete, and a serious, contemplative student; not someone people would expect to take drugs. But he did.

On a Saturday night in May 2014, Sam and his two best friends were having a sleepover and decided to try N-Bomb. They contacted a dealer, bought the drug, and used it—and the next morning, Sam's two friends found him dead. "It came out of the blue," says Motsay. "Sam was a health conscious kid who looked the other way when it came to teenage smokers and drinkers."[37] She realizes that she may never know why Sam took the drug. It could have been peer pressure, the desire to go along with his friends, or just a terribly bad decision that defies reason—one that cost him his life.

Brain Development in Progress

Although there are many reasons why teens make bad choices (such as using synthetic drugs), an important factor is adolescent brain development; specifically, that the brains of teenagers are not as developed as those of adults. "These brain differences don't mean that young people can't make good decisions or tell the difference between right and wrong," says the American Academy of Child and Adolescent Psychiatry. "It also doesn't mean that they shouldn't be held responsible for their actions. But an awareness of these differences can help parents, teachers, advocates, and policy makers understand, anticipate, and manage the behavior of adolescents."[38]

Years of research have been devoted to studying the human brain, with a special focus on the brains of adolescents. "The research has turned up some surprises," says the National Institute of Mental Health (NIMH), "among them the discovery of striking changes taking place during the teen years." Contrary to what scientists believed for years, it is now known that the brains of adolescents are not yet fully developed. "In key ways," says NIMH, "the brain doesn't look like that of an adult until the early 20s."[39]

Because of brain research, scientists now know that the brain develops from back to front, with the prefrontal cortex being the last part to develop. This is located at the very front of the brain behind the forehead, and it controls such functions as reasoning, problem solving, impulse control, and decision making. Teens are prone to impulsive, even risky behaviors largely due to the prefrontal cortex not being fully developed. "One interpretation of all these findings," says NIMH, "is that in teens, the parts of the brain involved in emotional responses are fully online, or even more active than in adults, while the parts of the brain involved in keeping emotional, impulsive responses in check are still reaching maturity. Such a changing balance might provide clues to a youthful appetite for novelty, and a tendency to act on impulse— without regard for risk."[40] In other words, young people who might normally be against taking drugs could be influenced by peer pressure and use drugs to appear "cool" or to just go along with what the crowd is doing.

How the brain grows and develops is the focus of neuroscientist Frances Jensen's book *The Teenage Brain*. Jensen explains the brain's growth process and describes the role played by an underdeveloped brain in bad decision making and impulsivity by teens. "Teenagers are not as readily able to access their frontal lobe to say, 'Oh, I better not do this,'" says Jensen. She goes on to explain that during the brain's development, cells slowly build myelin, a natural insulation that speeds the electrical impulses traveling throughout the central nervous system. "The last place to be connected—to be fully myelinated—is the front of your brain," she says. "And what's in the front? Your prefrontal cortex and your frontal cortex. These are areas where we have insight, empathy, these executive functions such as impulse control, risk-taking behavior."[41]

"In key ways, the brain doesn't look like that of an adult until the early 20s."[39]

— National Institute of Mental Health, the largest scientific organization in the world dedicated to the study of mental illness.

Trying to Cheat Drug Tests

Substance abuse experts and law enforcement professionals say that one of the biggest draws of synthetic cannabis (including for teens) is that it does not show up on standard drug tests. This came through clearly in a survey that appeared in the July 2014 issue of *Drug and Alcohol Dependence*. Of nearly four hundred participants who were asked why they used synthetic cannabis, 71 percent said because they could get high without having to worry about flunking a drug test. "People do use these compounds primarily to evade drug tests," says Kevin G. Shanks, a forensic toxicologist from Indianapolis, Indiana. "The typical urine drug test for cannabinoids does not pick up synthetic cannabinoids."

Shanks says this was not common knowledge until about 2012, but it is now widely known. So labs that perform drug testing need to have updated technology capable of testing for more than just metabolites of THC, the active ingredient in marijuana, which is not found in synthetic cannabis.

Quoted in Alison Knopf, "Deadly Synthetic Cannabinoids Used to Evade Marijuana Drug Tests," *Drug & Alcoholism Weekly*, September 15, 2014. www.alcoholismdrugabuseweekly.com.

High-Risk Teens

Through years of research, scientists have learned that brain development can be a significant factor in the types of choices teens make. But many other factors also come into play, such as gender, family upbringing, home environment, substance abuse history, friends, and social life. Identifying the risk factors involved when teens use synthetic drugs is the focus of a major 2014 study by New York University researcher Joseph J. Palamar and colleagues. Palamar acknowledges that use of synthetic cannabis among teens began to decline in 2014. Still, however, the drug has been associated

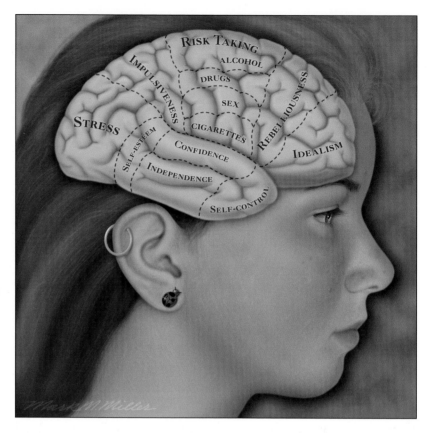

The adolescent brain is a still-developing organ. As the brain develops so does the ability to reason, solve problems, control impulses, and make decisions.

with tens of thousands of adverse effects and hospitalizations, especially among teens. He writes: "It is important to examine which teens are at highest risk for use of these new, potentially deleterious drugs as they are understudied and continue to emerge."[42]

During the study the researchers examined numerous factors that could potentially influence a teen's decision whether to use (or not use) synthetic cannabis. One of the factors was gender: Boys were consistently more likely to use the drug than girls. Race was also a factor, with black students 42 percent less likely to use synthetic cannabis than white teens. Also, teens who go out for fun four or more nights per week were found to have a high risk for experimenting with synthetic cannabis and to continue using it. "More research is needed," says Palamar, "but this may be due to increased exposure to others who use these products during these nightly activities."[43]

The strongest risk factor for using synthetic cannabis was

the use of other substances such as alcohol, cigarettes, and illicit drugs. The study found that drinking alcohol at any time in their lives nearly doubled the teens' odds that they would use synthetic cannabis. Regular cigarette smoking (past or present) more than doubled the odds. By far the greatest risk was to teens who had used marijuana at some point. "All levels of lifetime marijuana use robustly increased the odds for use," says Palamar, "and as frequency of marijuana use increased, odds for use of synthetic cannabinoids increased."[44]

A Vexing Problem

Because synthetic drugs are still relatively new, little research has been done to pinpoint exactly why teens are drawn to them. From surveys, interviews with teens, feedback from health care providers, and research that examined why teens use other types of drugs, experts have concluded that a number of factors could play a role. These include gender, low awareness of the risks involved in using synthetic drugs, deceptive marketing tactics, and poor decision-making skills associated with teenagers' brains not being fully developed. As Palamar's 2015 study shows, previous or current marijuana use is a very strong factor associated with use of synthetic drugs. As research continues scientists will likely learn more about why teens use these substances, and this could potentially lead to better prevention efforts.

"As frequency of marijuana use increased, odds for use of synthetic cannabinoids increased."[44]

— Joseph J. Palamar, a researcher with New York University.

Facts

- According to Cupertino, California–based CRC Health Group, teens who struggle with mental health issues or behavioral disorders may use drugs as a misguided attempt to self-medicate.

- Health and law enforcement officials say that people who use flakka are attracted to the price, which is much lower than for other types of stimulants.

- A 2015 study led by New York researcher Joseph J. Palamar found that more than 14 percent of teens who had drunk alcohol also tried synthetic cannabis, compared with only 1.2 percent of teens who had never drunk alcohol.

- According to Stephanie Siete, a drug outreach coordinator in Phoenix, Arizona, the number one reason teens use synthetic drugs is boredom.

- A January 2014 report by the DEA cites a study of men aged thirty or younger, of whom 39 percent who had used synthetic cannabinoids passed a traditional drug screen test.

- According to the Partnership for Drug-Free Kids, teens who smoke synthetic cannabinoids get high in three to five minutes, and the high can last up to eight hours.

What Are the Dangers of Synthetic Drug Use?

During the early months of 2015 Broward County, Florida, was the site of some of the most bizarre synthetic drug incidents law enforcement had ever seen. Reports began to surface about a drug called flakka, or gravel, as it is sometimes known. Flakka is a synthetic cathinone that is cousin to bath salts but is far more potent and longer lasting. It contains a powerful synthetic stimulant called alpha-Pyrrolidinopentiophenone (alpha-PVP)—and when people use it, many behave as though they have lost their minds. "It's just a nasty, nasty drug," says Timothy Heiser, who is deputy fire chief in Fort Lauderdale, the county seat of Broward County. Heiser goes on to say that flakka turns users into "nasty people and dangerous people."[45]

"$5 Insanity"

When people use flakka, either by snorting, smoking, or liquefying for injection into a vein, one of the most common effects is called "excited delirium." This is a frightening, potentially dangerous condition during which someone high on the drug becomes hyperstimulated, aggressive, and often violent. Users often become psychotic and lose all connection with reality, which leads to hallucinations: seeing people or creatures that do not really exist, or even more common, hearing voices. Flakka-induced psychosis can also cause delusions, which are strange, irrational beliefs about events or circumstances that have actually not taken place. For instance, users may become convinced that they are being watched or chased or feeling certain that someone (or something) is out to get them.

During these fits of excited delirium, body temperature can soar to a dangerously high 106 degrees Fahrenheit (41.1°C), which is a condition known as hyperthermia. People have been known to rip their clothes off in public in a desperate attempt to find relief from being unbearably hot. "They strip off their clothes and run outdoors, acting very violent with adrenaline-surged strength," says Jim Hall, an epidemiologist (disease expert) at Nova Southeastern University in Fort Lauderdale. "It can take four or more cops to hold them down."[46] According to Hall, an abnormally high body temperature can be life-threatening. One danger is the breakdown of muscle tissue, which in turn allows muscle fiber to be released into the bloodstream. This can result in severe damage to the kidneys as well as kidney failure. Another risk is heart attack due to a surging heart rate and brain damage that may be permanent.

Another effect of excited delirium is to be overcome by severe paranoia. This can be all-consuming and horrifying to those affected by it—so much so that they will do anything to escape from the imagined threat. Fort Lauderdale drug treatment and addiction counselor Don Maines says that people high on flakka become seriously paranoid. "They can't think straight . . . they think people are chasing them," he says. "One guy thought he was surrounded by German Shepherds that were attacking him."[47]

Maines goes on to say that even some who use flakka regularly are terrified of it. "I had one addict describe it as $5 insanity," he says. "They still want to try it because it's so cheap. It gives them heightened awareness. They feel stronger and more sensitive to touch. But then the paranoia sets in. . . . They have no control over their thoughts. They can't control their actions. It seems to

"[Flakka users] strip off their clothes and run outdoors, acting very violent with adrenaline-surged strength."[46]

— Jim Hall, an epidemiologist at Nova Southeastern University in Fort Lauderdale, Florida.

be universal that they think someone is chasing them. It's just a dangerous, dangerous drug."[48]

Bedlam in Broward County

One of the first flakka cases in Fort Lauderdale occurred in February 2015 when fifty-year-old James West smoked the drug and started hallucinating. He ran toward the police station for help, convinced that he was being chased by a mob of people. When West arrived at the police station and found the doors locked, he was frantic, feeling desperate to get inside to escape from his "followers." He grabbed the door handles and started shaking the doors, trying to force them open, and then he repeatedly kicked at the doors. When they still would not budge, West grabbed rocks and started bashing the hurricane-resistant glass, managing to crack it.

Although West had gone to the police station for help, he became paranoid when he saw police officers and took off running. They captured him in the parking lot and drove him to the hospital, where emergency room physician Nabil El Sanadi treated him. El Sanadi was fairly certain about what drug West had taken because his behavior was similar to several other recent flakka cases. The doctor says that hallucinations are common among people who take the drug, and they can incite fear and desperation. "The drug is stimulating their brain," says El Sanadi, "making them think there may be people chasing them, people after them, maybe the devil is trying to get them, take their heart out."[49]

"I had one addict describe [flakka] as ⅓ s insanity."[48]

— Don Maines, drug treatment and addiction counselor in Fort Lauderdale, Florida.

One of the most cringeworthy Fort Lauderdale cases occurred one month after the James West incident. Thirty-eight-year-old Shanard Neely smoked flakka, and like West became severely paranoid. Convinced that murderers were after him, Neely ran toward the police station to get help and scaled a tall metal security fence around the perimeter. He planned to jump over the fence—but his plan went seriously awry. When he mounted the 14-foot (4.27m) gate, he lost his balance and fell on one of the wrought iron security spikes that line the top. The spike drove into Neely's thigh

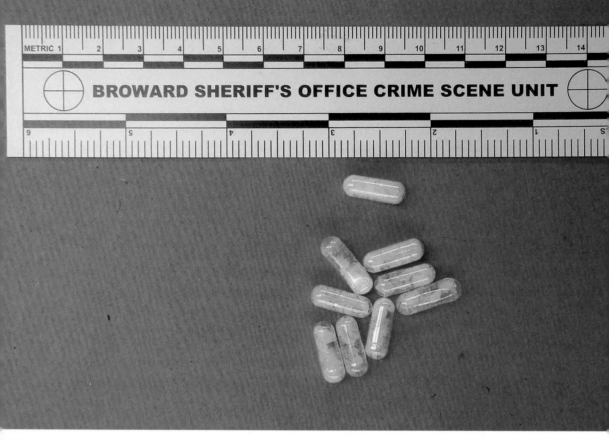

METRIC 1 2 3 4 5 6 7 8 9 10 11 12 13 14

BROWARD SHERIFF'S OFFICE CRIME SCENE UNIT

Confiscated capsules of flakka are displayed in the Broward County (Florida) sheriff's office. One of the newest synthetic drugs, flakka can dangerously alter brain chemistry in users.

near his crotch and came out the back through his buttocks. Firefighters refueling a truck nearby heard him screaming and were horrified to see him hanging on the fence, impaled by the spike.

With great care, rescuers used special tools to free Neely by cutting the iron spike away from the fence. The rescue took several hours, and with the spike still in his body, he was transported to the hospital. "It was a very delicate ride to the hospital," says Heiser. "You think it's bad enough to have a fence impaled in you, but then if you don't have people skilled enough and trained to treat you properly, you're one sneeze away from possibly bleeding to death or having permanent damage."[50] Doctors performed emergency surgery on Neely to remove the spike. Miraculously, it had not pierced any major arteries, and he was expected to make a full recovery.

Unpredictable and Unsafe

Synthetic cannabis is not the same as flakka, but users can also experience a number of bad effects, including paranoia. One of the biggest myths about synthetic cannabis (which many young people believe) is that it is like marijuana but made in a laboratory. In fact, the only characteristic Spice and marijuana have in common is that both drugs bind to cannabinoid receptors in the brain. Beyond that, it is a dangerous misconception that synthetic cannabis is marijuana made by humans. "This stuff is so bad," says Spencer Greene, an emergency room physician and director of medical toxicology at the Baylor College of Medicine in Houston, Texas. "It is not anything like marijuana."[51]

According to the NIDA, scientists now know that some of the compounds found in synthetic cannabinoids bind more strongly than THC to cannabinoid receptors. This could help explain why people who smoke Spice experience a much more powerful and unpredictable effect than what they may expect. Also, synthetic cannabinoids can differ dramatically from one package to the next, as Clay Brown, director of adolescent services at Memorial Hermann Prevention and Recovery Center in Houston explains, "One day you might get a pretty good buzz and two days later you buy it and end up . . . completely psychotic. They have chest pains, think they are having a heart attack. They are tearing their clothes off, screaming obscenities, biting themselves and attacking people."[52]

Brown's mention of people high on Spice becoming "psychotic" refers to those who have lost touch with reality—meaning they cannot tell what is real from what is imagined. This is when delusions or hallucinations occur, and it is a dangerous, erratic state. John W. Huffman recalls learning about a particularly tragic case of someone who was high on the drug and suffered a psychotic break. "A few years ago I gave a live interview to Russian TV and was told about a young woman who had smoked Spice, presumably containing JWH-018," says Huffman. "She hallucinated and thought that she could fly. Unfortunately, she was on the 10th floor of the building."[53]

Breanna Phebus, a young woman from Southern California, started using Spice because she could buy it at local smoke shops rather than having to deal with a drug dealer. "I had no idea what I

"This stuff is so bad. It is not anything like marijuana."[51]

— Spencer Greene, an emergency room physician and director of medical toxicology at the Baylor College of Medicine in Houston.

was getting into," she says, "and as soon as I did it, I was hooked."[54] When Phebus thinks about all the times she smoked Spice to get high, she is overcome with bad memories. About a particularly bad episode, she recalls, "Oh my God, terrifying." She flooded the house and had no memory of what happened. Another time she woke up and found holes in all the walls. Once after getting high on Spice, Phebus fell through a glass table and cut herself severely. "It was just a rampage for days of not knowing what you're doing,"

Too Young to Die

Health officials want desperately to get across how unpredictable synthetic drugs are. Users have no way of knowing how potent the drugs are or whether they will cause a physical reaction—one that could be fatal. There are multiple reports of people taking the same drug at the same time, and one of them dies. This was the case in November 2014, when a group of teenagers from Springfield, Missouri, smoked synthetic cannabis. Two of the teens were fourteen-year-old Shaylee Marsh and thirteen-year-old Ealiesha Tyler. "They passed it around, it got to me, I hit it three times," says Marsh. "And Ealiesha did the same."

Marsh immediately felt the effects of the drug and remarked that she was high. Tyler just stared at her, shaking his head, and she saw that he looked pale. "That's the last thing I remember," says Marsh. She passed out, and when she regained consciousness she learned that Tyler had died. "I feel very responsible because I am a year older than him, and I am the one that passed it to him," she says. "And it hurts me a lot because I feel like it's my fault that he's dead now because I gave him the K2. I didn't supply it, but I did hand it to him. And I shouldn't have."

Quoted in Rachel Dubrovin, "Teens Caution Community About the Dangers of K-2," KSPR, November 6, 2014. www.kspr.com.

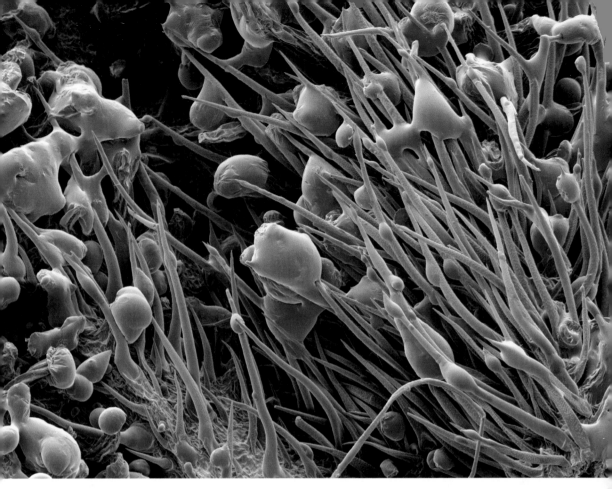

A scanning electron micrograph provides a close-up view of THC drug crystals that are found in marijuana. The compounds found in synthetic cannabinoids bind more strongly to cannabinoid receptors in the brain than does THC.

she says. "It's something unexplainable . . . it was just the worst vicious cycle that took me to the depths of hell."[55]

As painful and frightening as her experiences with Spice were, Phebus candidly talks to young people about it. Her hope is that they will avoid making the same mistakes she did. She tells them, "I remember . . . the feeling of dying alone and in the dark and out of my mind. Take it from an addict, you don't want to be me. But it's never too late to quit."[56]

The Scourge of Addiction

Phebus admits that she became hopelessly addicted to Spice, and research has shown this to be true of many other people as well. According to the accounts of users who became hooked on synthetic drugs, they are some of the most addictive substances of all time. As the popularity of synthetic drugs continues to grow, substance abuse experts fear that addiction to the drugs will increase accordingly. Marilyn Huestis explains, "It's estimated that one in 10 people who try marijuana develop problematic use. But it's been well-documented that designer drugs are up to 100 times more potent, so we know that individuals are becoming dependent on them as well."[57]

A teenager from Newport News, Virginia, became seriously addicted to synthetic cannabis after being a regular marijuana user. He was still in middle school when he started smoking marijuana. "Weed was just part of life," he says. "I smoked weed all the time—after school, every weekend."[58] When he was in the eighth grade he started smoking Spice, which like many teens he considered to be a synthetic version of marijuana. It was attractive because it was cheaper than marijuana, much easier to purchase (at smoke shops, rather than having to find a dealer), and was not detectable on drug tests. What the teen never anticipated, however, was that he would become addicted to the drug.

Before long he found that he could not function without it. He smoked Spice before school in the morning, in the bathroom during the school day, and at home before he went to bed at night. He was so hooked on the drug that he would do most anything to get it, including stealing money from his parents and pawning their possessions to get more money. Finally he was given a choice: Go to rehab or go to jail, and he chose the former. Now eighteen years old and drug-free for nearly two years, the teen despises synthetic cannabis. "The smell makes me sick to my stomach," he says. "It's nasty stuff."[59]

Forever Changed

The Newport News teen put himself and his family through unbearable pain, which he now deeply regrets. But he was fortunate enough to recover from his addiction without any permanent damage to his health. The same cannot be said of Emily Bauer, a teenager from Cypress, Texas. Because of a serious reaction to Spice in 2012, Bauer's life will never be the same.

The incident happened when Bauer was a sophomore in high

Tragic Deception

Even though synthetic cannabinoids and cathinones have only existed for a relatively short period of time, they have proved to be among the most unpredictable and dangerous drugs in existence. But some older synthetic drugs that are not so well known have also proved to be dangerous. The powerful synthetic painkilling drug fentanyl, for example, was created in 1960 by Paul Janssen, a pharmacist from Belgium. Janssen was hailed for his contributions to medical science—but during the 1970s some unscrupulous individuals introduced his creation into the illicit marketplace. Fentanyl was distributed to heroin addicts who had no idea that the drug they were buying was exponentially more potent than heroin. In a September 2013 statement before the US Senate, the DEA's Joseph T. Rannazzisi explained:

> Drug abusers were the unknowing test subjects used to determine the viability of the substances as a replacement for controlled narcotics. This uncontrolled experimentation resulted in overdose deaths in concentrated areas of the country with law enforcement authorities scrambling to identify the drug and locate the clandestine laboratories and chemists that produced the substances. In some instances, it wasn't the strength of the drug, but its toxic contaminants that ultimately harmed the users.

Joseph T. Rannazzisi, "Statement Before the Caucus on International Narcotics Control, United States Senate for a Hearing Entitled, 'Dangerous Synthetic Drugs,'" Drug Enforcement Agency, September 25, 2013. www.dea.gov.

school. Without her parents' knowledge she had smoked Spice for a couple weeks and enjoyed the way it made her feel. But on December 7, 2012, something felt different after she smoked it. After just a few hits, Bauer developed a splitting headache and told her family she was going to lie down for a nap—and when she woke up, it was like she had morphed into a ranting, raving stranger.

Bauer was stumbling around the house, trying to talk but slurring her words, screaming at everyone, hallucinating, and behaving violently. Her parents called 911, and paramedics arrived, strapped her to a gurney, and rushed her to the hospital. Bauer screamed and flailed her arms, biting the guardrails and trying to bite medical personnel who were attempting to help her. She was so out of her mind that she had to be strapped to the bed. Her family and doctors hoped that she would be better in the morning, but twenty-four hours later there was no improvement in her condition. Bauer was still psychotic as well as violent, so doctors put her into a medically induced coma. Several days later brain scans showed that Bauer had suffered several serious strokes, which had caused bleeding on the brain and devastating brain damage. Doctors said there was no hope for the teen to ever recover; she would likely never function on her own or even recognize her family. So, her parents made the decision to remove Bauer from life support.

The doctors were wrong, however. To everyone's shock, Bauer woke up, smiled at her mother, and whispered that she loved her. She started making slow but steady progress, and in September 2013 she returned to her high school. As of April 2015 Bauer is still confined to a wheelchair, is partially blind, and has many physical and mental challenges. Yet she is thankful to be alive and is determined to work hard and make progress at being more independent. "I believe I will walk again and have a full recovery," says Bauer. "I want people to know drugs are bad and the effects are horrible."[60]

Young Lives Wasted

Many people would agree that synthetic drugs are horrible—especially the families of young people who have been injured or have died because of them. One of the worst aspects of these drugs is that so much remains unknown about them. Because they are so unpredictable, with potency that can vary dramatically from

David Rozga, pictured in the photograph held by his parents and brother, was starting to make plans for college in 2010. At a get-together with friends, he smoked K2; under the drug's influence, he later shot himself to death.

one package to the next, there is no way for users to know how the drugs will affect their brains. Health officials and substance abuse experts say that one of the gravest risks of ingesting these chemicals is that users lose their ability to think clearly and rationally. This can potentially lead to feelings of hopelessness and possibly suicide. There are numerous cases of young people who took their own lives after using synthetic drugs, and with many of them, it was completely unexpected and shocking.

This was the case with eighteen-year-old David Rozga from Indianola, Iowa. A healthy, happy, athletic teen, Rozga graduated from high school in June 2010 and was starting to make plans to attend college in the fall. During a get-together with some friends, one of the teens brought out a packet of the synthetic cannabinoid K2 that was purchased at a novelty store in a local shopping mall. Thinking it would give him the mellow high of marijuana, Rozga smoked the drug—and immediately his friends could tell that something was very wrong. He was acting crazy and agitated, as though he were having severe panic attacks. Then he started to hallucinate, telling his friends that he felt like he was in hell. A short while later Rozga seemed to calm down a little, and he told his friends he was tired and was going home to sleep. He did go home; but when he got there, he found a rifle in the house and shot himself to death.

Mark Ryan says that during his seventeen years as director of the Louisiana Poison Center he has heard just about everything, so very little surprises him anymore. But when he heard about David Rozga's senseless death, it hit him especially hard. "As David's mother described to me the circumstances surrounding his death I felt sick," says Ryan. "It was obvious that what these new drugs did to users was extremely dangerous, but at that point I wasn't sure if or how we could stop it from happening again. We know more now, and we've made progress—but we still have a very long way to go."[61]

Vast Unknowns, Inconceivable Risk

Whether they are smoked, snorted, taken in pill form, injected, or allowed to melt on the tongue, synthetic drugs are potent, dangerous, and unpredictable. They have not been around long enough for scientists to conduct long-term research, but there are enough cases of injury and death to predict that the drugs are bad news. "This new generation of young people needs to know this stuff can kill you," says Carol Falkowski, an epidemiology specialist and CEO of Drug Abuse Dialogues in St. Paul, Minnesota. "It's really a game of Russian roulette."[62]

Facts

- According to a winter 2015 report by the Prevention Resource Center in Lubbock, Texas, 27 percent of teens who use synthetic cannabinoids experience dizziness and nausea, 18 percent experience panic, and 15 percent suffer from headaches.

- An October 2014 SAMHSA report shows that teens and young adults aged twelve to twenty-nine accounted for 79 percent of 2011 emergency room visits related to synthetic cannabinoid use.

- According to NIDA director Nora D. Volkow, teens who use bath salts risk developing high blood pressure, rapid heart rate, agitation, hallucinations, extreme paranoia, and delusions.

- Health officials in South Florida reported in April 2015 that hospitals were admitting twenty new patients per day for problems related to the use of the synthetic cathinone flakka.

- On April 16, 2015, New York governor Andrew M. Cuomo issued a health alert saying that an increase in the use of synthetic cannabinoids caused more than 160 people to be hospitalized in a nine-day period.

- In April 2015 more than four hundred emergency room visits in Mississippi were attributed to synthetic cannabinoids, according to the state health department.

What Legal Challenges Are Associated with Synthetic Drugs?

O
n March 4, 2015, a flight from Beijing, China, arrived at Los Angeles International Airport. Such an occurrence is not out of the ordinary; Air China flies into the same airport multiple times each week. But this particular flight carried a Chinese passenger named Haijun Tian, whose arrival DEA agents had been anticipating. A grand jury had indicted the thirty-three-year-old Tian for running one of the world's largest synthetic cannabinoid manufacturing operations. His indictment was the culmination of a three-year investigation called Operation Poisyn Control, which involved the DEA, the Internal Revenue Service's Criminal Investigation division, and US Immigration and Customs Enforcement (ICE). As soon as Tian emerged from the jetway, DEA agents surrounded him and placed him under arrest.

On the Trail of a Drug Kingpin

US law enforcement officials have long known that China is the world's largest hub for the manufacture and export of chemicals used to make synthetic drugs. This knowledge was reinforced by the discovery of Tian's operation, which was churning out extraordinary amounts of synthetic cannabinoids each year. According to *New York Times* national correspondent Alan Schwarz, Tian's arrest "underscores rising concerns that China, with its large and poorly regulated pharmaceutical sector, could become to spice what Colombia or Peru has been for cocaine, or Afghanistan is to heroin."[63]

In the early days of Operation Poisyn Control, the DEA decided that the best way to get to Tian was through one of his biggest wholesale customers. A summer 2012 raid on a synthetic cannabinoid manufacturing facility in Tampa, Florida, yielded a

Web of Drugs

There are extraordinary challenges involved with trying to curtail the spread of synthetic drugs, and one of the most formidable is regulating Internet sales. As law enforcement officials have clamped down on retail stores that sell the drugs, buyers have increasingly turned to the Internet—and with hundreds of millions of websites, keeping track of online drug dealers is close to impossible.

In May 2014, after her twenty-two-year-old son, Philip, died from smoking synthetic cannabis, Elizabeth Manning made a shocking discovery. On his laptop she saw a link to The Happy Chemist, a Chinese company that purportedly sold "research chemicals" but offered vivid descriptions of how they made users feel. It soon became obvious that Philip had been buying chemicals directly from the site and making his own brand of Spice. "He got it just like you'd go online and get a book," says Manning. "You buy something but you don't know what it is, and it could be poison."

Quoted in Alan Schwarz, "Arrest Underscores China's Role in the Making and Spread of a Lethal Drug," *New York Times*, May 28, 2015. www.nytimes.com.

massive amount of contraband. According to the DEA, agents seized "thousands of kilograms of processed smokable cannabinoid products, approximately 200 kilograms of raw synthetic cannabinoid compound, a variety of firearms and in excess of $750,000."[64] The DEA later learned that the raw synthetic cannabinoids used in the manufacturing facility came from China, and most were supplied by Tian. Agents identified the operation's wholesaler/distributor who had been purchasing the raw chemicals in powder form as far back as 2011. They tracked him down in Wisconsin and arrested him. When agents offered him an opportunity to be a confidential informant for the DEA, the man accepted.

DEA officials instructed him to send an e-mail to Tian. In the e-mail the man would inquire about the availability and price of a synthetic cannabinoid known as AB-FUBINACA (ABF), which had recently been added to the DEA's list of controlled substances. As directed, the informant sent an e-mail to Tian saying, "The U.S. government made ABF illegal a few days ago, but I still have a couple of people who want to buy some if the price is good. Do you have any ABF left over? How much would you sell it for?"[65] Tian replied immediately, saying that he did have the drug in stock, and in a separate e-mail he quoted a price of $900 per kilogram.

Tian shipped several packages of ABF to the informant in Wisconsin, and then traveled to Los Angeles where he was apprehended by DEA agents at the airport. He was indicted for manufacturing AB-FUBINACA in China knowing that he would be unlawfully importing it into the United States, and for importing an illegal substance into the United States. As of late June 2015 Tian was in a Wisconsin jail awaiting trial. If convicted he faces up to sixty years in prison and a $3 million fine.

Drug Control

Tian's apprehension was a major coup for the DEA. In a May 2015 news release the agency refers to him as the "highest-level synthetic designer drug trafficker apprehended to date in the United States."[66] During prior sting operations, which have also been carefully and strategically planned, DEA agents have successfully tracked down and arrested numerous other high-level syn-

thetic drug manufacturers and distributors. A synthetic drug take-down called Project Synergy, for instance, resulted in more than 227 arrests and 416 search warrants served in thirty-five states, forty-nine cities, and five countries, as well as seizure of more than $60 million in cash and assets.

Yet despite these and other triumphs, trying to stop the manu-facture, sale, and use of synthetic drugs has proved to be a for-midable challenge for law enforcement. Once the drugmakers discovered the scientific formulas and used them to start creating drugs, they seemed impossible to shut down—largely because so many people were buying the products. "Is it frustrating? Yes," says Keith Brown, special agent in charge of the DEA field office in New Orleans, Louisiana. "But when you're in this business what you come to understand is that total eradication of a drug threat just isn't going to happen. Until we can control the demand there's going to be someone with supply."[67]

Pharmaceutical workers in China package drugs for sale around the world. US law enforcement agencies say that China is the global center for manufacturing and exporting chemicals used in synthetic drugs.

In the United States the grandfather of drug legislation is the Controlled Substances Act (CSA), which was signed into law by President Richard M. Nixon in 1970. The CSA regulates the manufacture, possession, distribution, and use of certain drugs and substances. The law also covers precursor chemicals, which are ingredients that are used to make drugs. For instance, an oxidizing chemical called potassium permanganate is a precursor for producing synthetic cathinones, which are controlled substances in the United States.

The CSA categorizes drugs and other substances into five schedules (or classifications), depending on criteria such as medicinal value, potential for abuse and/or addiction, and safety. Schedule I drugs (such as Ecstasy, LSD, heroin, and marijuana) are those that are considered harmful, have a high potential for abuse and/or addiction, and have been declared to have no accepted medical use in the United States. Schedules II to V descend from there; Schedule V drugs are the least harmful, with little or no potential for abuse or addiction.

Making the Law Work Better

The CSA was amended twice in the years after it became law. The first amendment was in 1984 with passage of the Crime Control Act. Also referred to as *emergency scheduling*, the law holds that the US attorney general has the power to schedule substances on a temporary basis, meaning to designate the substances as Schedule I. The attorney general delegates this power to the DEA, which follows clearly defined protocol for scheduling. For instance, to temporarily schedule a substance, it must meet the scheduling requirements outlined in the CSA.

Also required for a substance to be temporarily scheduled is for the DEA to examine eight factors as listed in the CSA and determine that three of the eight factors exist. "Last," says the National Association of Attorneys General (NAAG), "the agencies must also determine that the scheduling is necessary to 'avoid imminent hazards to public safety.'"[68] Once a substance has been temporarily scheduled it may remain on the controlled substances list for two years and possibly an additional year. When the time is up the DEA makes a determination about whether it should be permanently scheduled.

The second amendment to the CSA was in 1986 with passage of the Controlled Substances Analogue Enforcement Act, or Analogue Act as it is commonly known. This law expanded the CSA to include bans on drug analogues, which are substances that are chemically similar to banned drugs. The law defines analogues based on three factors: the chemical structure is close to the chemical structure of a controlled substance; the drug's effect on the central nervous system is the same or greater than the effect of a controlled substance; and the producer's intent that the drug will have a stimulant, depressant, or hallucinogenic effect on the user. Thus, the Analogue Act served as a method of criminalizing drugs without having to ban each of the drugs individually by scheduling them.

Tougher Approach Needed

Together, the CSA and Analogue Act served as the United States' major drug legislation throughout the 1980s, the 1990s, and into the twenty-first century. Seldom during that period of time did the DEA have to use its emergency scheduling authority. Then in February 2011, when synthetic drugs were growing into a serious problem throughout the United States, the DEA used its emergency power to temporarily ban five synthetic cannabinoids. With that action it became illegal to manufacture, distribute, possess, import, or export the banned substances. Seven months later, in October 2011, the DEA used its emergency power again to temporarily add three synthetic cathinones to the Schedule I list of banned substances.

Even with these actions, however, it was becoming abundantly clear that a much more comprehensive, wide-reaching solution was needed. The synthetic drugmakers were introducing new drugs each week, and law enforcement personnel were overwhelmed. "If we can make the bad guys react to what we're doing instead of us reacting to what the bad guys are doing," says DEA agent James Burns, "then I think that'll help us get a better handle on this issue."[69]

"If we can make the bad guys react to what we're doing instead of us reacting to what the bad guys are doing, then I think that'll help us get a better handle on this issue."[69]

— James Burns, a DEA agent in New York State.

The Price of Deception

For law enforcement one of the biggest challenges in trying to stop synthetic drug abuse is monitoring the retail stores that continue to sell them. Throughout the country sting operations have revealed that tobacco shops, head shops, and other stores stock the drugs, skirting the law with product disclaimers such as *Not for human consumption*. So, some states are using a creative approach to catch and prosecute the retailers.

In February 2015 a judge in Des Moines, Iowa, ordered the owners of a convenience store to pay $50,000 to the state and barred them from selling synthetic substances. This was the culmination of a first-of-its-kind consumer protection lawsuit filed by Iowa's attorney general. It was filed after an undercover narcotics officer visited the store (Shop 'n Save) and purchased a package of 7H. Although it was labeled *aromatic potpourri*, the store clerk provided the officer with a glass smoking pipe to be used while inhaling the contents of the package. Later, during a search of the business, police seized nearly one thousand packages of synthetic cannabis: Caution, Kush, OMG, Scooby Snax, and Stardust, as well as 7H. Despite all the products being labeled *Not FDA approved* and *Not fit for human consumption*, the lawsuit stated that they were drugs and were indeed for human consumption. When the judge agreed, the attorney general said in his statement: "We sincerely hope that holding these sellers accountable will send a strong message to other retailers who think it's worth the risk to sell synthetic drugs here in Iowa."

Quoted in *North Iowa Today*, "Judge Bars Iowa Convenience Store Owners from Selling Synthetic Drugs, Orders $50,000 Penalty," February 4, 2015. http://northiowatoday.com.

The US Congress began to discuss and debate legislation that specifically addressed synthetic drugs. After months of debating and negotiating, in July 2012 the Synthetic Drug Abuse Prevention Act was signed into law by President Barack Obama. The act, which took effect the following October, lengthened the period of time that a drug could be temporarily scheduled. It also permanently banned fifteen synthetic cannabinoids, two synthetic cathinones, and nine 2C hallucinogens by adding them to the list of Schedule I substances. Soon after the law was in place, John Parr, counsel to the US attorney in the Northern District of West Virginia, touted its advantages. "For prosecution purposes, the Synthetic Act provides great benefits," says Parr.

> By moving these substances from the analogue realm by making them scheduled controlled substances, prosecutors will not need to address the hurdles of "intended for human consumption" or of Chemistry 101 and dealing with chemical structures and pharmacological effect on the central nervous system. Rather, like every other drug case, simply proving the drug is what it is.[70]

Molecules Matter

As optimistic as Parr's outlook was at the time he made the statement, the phrase *human consumption* did indeed become a prosecutorial issue. Synthetic drug manufacturers have worked hard to skirt drug laws by intentionally marking their packages *Not for human consumption*. Even though that phrase is obviously being used fraudulently and the substance is indeed intended for human consumption, proving that in court is not nearly as simple as it may sound. NAAG writes:

> For example, to prove that a defendant possessed a drug listed in the CSA, such as cocaine, a prosecutor simply must show simple possession, and that the chemical makeup of the substance possessed was identical to that of cocaine. In contrast, to prove that a defendant possessed a cocaine analogue, a prosecutor must show a substantial similarity among the chemical structures of cocaine and

Ecstasy (pictured with other drugs) is classified as a Schedule I substance. These drugs are considered harmful and have a high potential for abuse.

the substance at issue, the effect that the substance at issue has on the central nervous system, and that *the defendant intended that the drug be intended for human consumption.*[71]

One of the most difficult challenges for the DEA and other law enforcement agencies is how quickly synthetic drugs can change as soon as they have been scheduled. One that is banned today might become a completely different drug next week—and technically it will be legal because its name is not on a controlled substances list. This happens when unscrupulous chemists deliberately make changes in their drug formulas to get around the controlled substance laws. "As soon as we make these things illegal, criminal organizations will go back and change one molecule . . . one molecule and it changes the entire drug," says James Capra, former DEA chief of operations. "It changes the whole structure of the drug, so the drug becomes legal and we're at it again. And that's the dynamic of what we're faced with."[72]

Mark Ryan agrees that the difficulties associated with synthetic drug legislation can seem insurmountable. He uses a metaphor when referring to the challenge of trying to keep a step ahead of the drug manufacturers and distributors: "It's like that arcade game Whac-A-Mole," says Ryan. "Whenever the mole sticks his head up you hit him, but he keeps popping up there, there, and there. That's what this is like—you're trying to whack a new synthetic drug that pops up and just when you've whacked it, another one pops up somewhere else."[73]

States Take Action

Ryan was the first poison center director to identify synthetic cathinones and build a comprehensive database. He was also instrumental in Louisiana becoming the first state to ban the substances. One by one other states followed, banning synthetic cannabinoids and cathinones. Many states had laws in place before the federal Synthetic Drug Abuse Prevention Act was signed into law. For instance, in March 2010 Kansas became the first state to ban synthetic cannabinoids by declaring JWH-018 and JWH-073 to be Schedule I drugs.

According to the National Conference on State Legislatures (NCSL), as of January 2015 all fifty states had banned both substances. "Initially," says the NCSL, "state legislative action targeted specific versions of these drugs with individual bans. However, minor changes to the chemical composition of these substances can create new, but very similar, drugs not previously covered by law."[74] The NCSL goes on to say that in subsequent years states have tended toward legislation that was more general in nature. For instance, they target entire classes of substances or use broad language to describe the prohibited drugs rather than more narrow descriptions that could make the laws less effective.

Some states have addressed their synthetic drug problems using creative approaches. "A few states also have passed laws restricting marketing, display, labeling, and advertising of these substances," says the NCSL, "by utilizing consumer

"As soon as we make these things illegal, criminal organizations will go back and change one molecule . . . one molecule and it changes the entire drug."[72]

— James Capra, the DEA's former chief of operations.

protection laws or classifying these activities as deceptive trade practices. Where substances are not specifically banned, law enforcement and prosecutors have also creatively used existing provisions such as agricultural regulations, consumer protection laws, and public nuisance laws to prosecute those selling these drugs."[75]

Tennessee has tough synthetic drug legislation in place, and it is one of the states that has gotten creative in its fight against the drugs. According to a February 2015 report by the DEA, Tennessee legislators passed a law in 2012 that made the sale of synthetic cannabinoids a felony offense. To put extra teeth in the law, businesses accused of selling the drugs can be closed and padlocked under a public nuisance charge. During the summer of 2012, not long after the law was passed, the Nashville police department and the Tennessee Bureau of Investigation shut down eleven convenience markets in Nashville for allegedly selling synthetic cannabinoids. "A state court order provided that the markets be searched," says the DEA, "any contraband and monies related to illegal activity be seized, and that the stores be padlocked pending a court appearance."[76]

One of the businesses, First Discount Tobacco & Beer, was padlocked during the 2012 sting—and in February 2014 was again padlocked after selling synthetic drugs. The owners admitted selling a liquid form of synthetic cannabinoids that is designed to be used with electronic cigarettes (e-cigarettes). The bottles were labeled with names such as Relax and Maui Maui and sold for forty dollars each. This time the store would be closed for ninety days, and officials said it was likely that the owner would be forced out of business. Gene Donegan, a narcotics supervisor with Nashville Metro police, says the tougher law has been invaluable in reducing the sale of synthetic drugs. "It's dramatically slowed it down,"[77] he says.

Another state that has been aggressive about its synthetic drug laws is Illinois, and state officials have seen positive results from it. "Just two years ago," says reporter Jason Nevel, "you could get your hands on synthetic drugs in Illinois at the same time you pumped gas and picked up a candy bar from a convenience store. But since a ban went into effect in August [2012], officials say

"It's a worldwide epidemic. It's a very serious problem and it's not going away anytime soon."[80]

— Ira Reese, executive director of US Customs and Border Protection Laboratories and Scientific Services division.

the use of synthetic drugs has plummeted across the state."[78] Before the synthetic drug legislation Illinois was about even with the national average for emergency calls to its state poison center. By June 2013, when the law had been in place for about ten months, the number of calls had dropped to half the national average.

In April 2015 Illinois officials announced that they had toughened synthetic drug legislation even further. Senate Bill 1129 addresses the basic chemical structure of the drugs, as Illinois state senator Kyle McCarter explains: "The legal definition has been bypassed many times by one change in the formula to produce the new drug. What this bill does is make the entire chemical structure illegal, which gets in front of all the future variations of the synthetics known as 'cannabinoids' and 'cathinones' and makes them illegal."[79]

So Many Uncertainties

The legal challenges associated with synthetic drugs are many, varied, and extremely frustrating for law enforcement. A number of efforts have been employed to curtail the manufacture, distribution, and use of the drugs, including drawing on existing legislation, passing new, tougher laws, and going after major drugmakers. While these efforts have definitely been a step in the right direction and have yielded positive results, experts agree that more needs to be done—although what that means, no one can say for sure. About the only thing that is widely agreed upon is that ending the synthetic drug problem will be no easy task. "It's a worldwide epidemic," says Ira Reese, executive director of US Customs and Border Protection Laboratories and Scientific Services division. "It's a very serious problem and it's not going away anytime soon."[80]

Facts

- According to the DEA, Georgia has a law that allows categories of synthetic drugs to be banned even before the specific compound is added to the Georgia code.

- In February 2015 the Synthetic Abuse and Labeling of Toxic Substances Act of 2015 took effect; it was designed to simplify the process of controlling substances if they are found to be intended for human consumption.

- According to a January 2015 report by the National Conference of State Legislatures, thirty-four states have analogue laws in place.

- In July 2012, after the Synthetic Drug Abuse Prevention Act was signed into law, bath salts–related calls to US poison centers dropped from a high of 422 the previous June to 81.

- According to the White House Office of National Drug Control Policy, prior to 2010 synthetic cannabinoids were not controlled by state or federal laws.

What Can Be Done About Synthetic Drug Abuse?

F or years the effectiveness (or lack thereof) of the so-called war on drugs has been a major topic of debate. Initiated in the 1970s by then president Richard M. Nixon, this was an approach that involved legislation, law enforcement, and public information. Nixon referred to the war on drugs as a "frontal assault on our number one public enemy" that was designed to "wipe out drug abuse in America."[81] Whether this war has accomplished what the Nixon administration intended is highly subjective and often a matter of personal opinion. Two realities cannot be ignored, however: People of all ages and all walks of life continue to use drugs, and the focus on criminalizing drug possession and use has resulted in a burgeoning prison population. Now, with the myriad challenges associated with synthetic drugs, substance abuse experts, legal scholars, and many others are calling for a radically different strategy.

NAAG, which is composed of the chief legal and law enforcement officers from all fifty states, argues that a radically different approach to fighting synthetic drugs is warranted. In the May 2014 issue of the publication *NAAGazette*, the group makes this viewpoint clear: "It is almost universally agreed that we cannot continue to incarcerate our way out of the drug problem in this country. Nowhere is this truer than in the area of synthetic drugs."[82]

As the top law enforcement professionals, America's attorneys general do not deny the value and necessity of traditional drug-fighting strategies. But the group believes strongly that the synthetic drug problem requires a "multipronged approach," meaning a wide variety of different tactics. They write: "While law enforcement and scheduling legislation play a huge role in addressing this scourge, the complexities of the problem make prevention, education and treatment invaluable. Particular care must be taken to educate young adults, parents, first responders, healthcare workers, and retailers."[83] Parents play a crucial role in helping their children understand what synthetic drugs are and the dangers involved with using them—but parents are not often familiar enough with the drugs themselves to share their knowledge.

Using Grief for Good

This lack of familiarity has been shown on many occasions when parents have lost a son or daughter to synthetic drugs. They not only suffer from unbearable grief; they are also shocked and confused about how this could happen to their child. Many of these parents have spoken publicly about their loss, often admitting that they had no idea such drugs existed—and they certainly did not know how easy the drugs were to obtain. In the 2014 Monitoring the Future study, the total number of teens who used Spice declined between 2012 and 2013; still, about 11 percent of high school seniors admitted using the drug in the previous twelve months. "Parents must be made aware of the prevalence and widespread availability of these drugs," says NAAG, "and must have the ability to identify both the products and the symptoms associated with their use."[84]

Keith and Debbie Bjerk, a couple from Grand Forks, North Dakota, lost their eighteen-year-old son, Christian, in June 2012. He had been at a party with friends and took the synthetic hallucinogenic drug 2C-1-NBOME, better known as N-Bomb. He was found dead the next morning, and a police officer, who had also been Christian's youth football coach, had to break the news to the Bjerks. Today, they are the first to admit they were completely naive about synthetic drugs when Christian died. Once they found out what had caused his death, they had to look up information on the Internet because they knew nothing about it. "Until the death of our son," the Bjerks write, "we knew very little about synthetic designer drugs." The more research they did, however, the more disturbed they felt, as they explain:

> We have been horrified to learn about the serious in-juries, thousands of calls to poison control, increased emergency room visits, severe psychotic states and deaths that have resulted from their use and the inef-fective and outdated state and federal laws that made it possible for many of these drugs to be sold in retail stores and online. America is at war with synthetic drugs. Sadly, the majority of Americans don't know about synthetic drugs or that the war is in their own homes via the Internet or at the corner tobacco store.[85]

> *"Until the death of our son, we knew very little about synthetic designer drugs."*[85]
>
> — Keith and Debbie Bjerk, a couple from Grand Forks, North Dakota, whose eighteen-year-old son died after taking N-Bomb.

After Christian's death the Bjerks became activists, doing ev-erything they could to fight the spread of synthetic drugs and to build awareness about the dangers of the drugs. They have talked to teenagers, other parents, law enforcement personnel, legislators, and educators. They have attended the court hearings of synthetic drug distributors—including the hearing for the man who distrib-uted the drug that killed their son. They testified before the North Dakota board of Pharmacy and at state legislative hearings to get tougher synthetic drug laws passed. Thanks largely to their effort, a number of the drugs are now illegal in their state. "We miss our son beyond words," say the Bjerks, "and in his memory, we have fought for change to protect other lives."[86]

Justice for Landon

What the Bjerks have accomplished in their son's memory has helped them deal with their tragic loss, as well as to potentially save other young lives. This is happening throughout the United States,

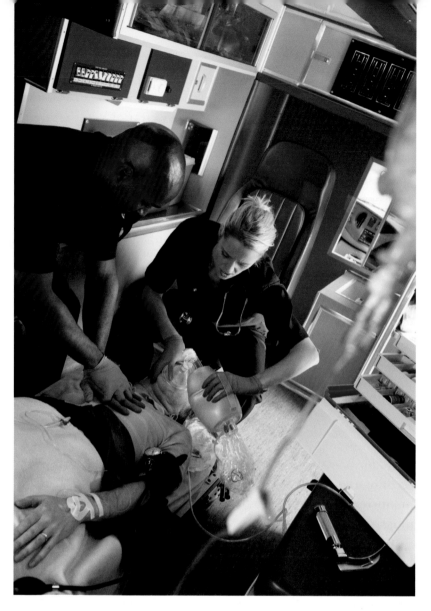

Paramedics perform CPR on a patient inside an ambulance. Not all first responders and emergency room personnel are familiar with the symptoms of synthetic drug use.

with parents and other family members working through their grief by working toward a cause. This is true of Chris and Juli Letsinger, a couple from Muscle Shoals, Alabama. In 2013 their seventeen-year-old son, Landon, also took N-bomb and immediately had a severe reaction to it. He stopped breathing and then his brain began to swell, and even though he was rushed to the hospital there was nothing doctors could do. Landon died eight days later.

Like Christian Bjerk's parents, the Letsingers knew almost nothing about synthetic drugs—but they vowed to change that after one of the drugs killed their son. They began working toward saving other young people from the same fate and also to save other families from having to go through what they went through. Says Juli Letsinger: "I wish young people would realize it just takes one time to have disastrous results and to realize how dangerous it is."[87]

The Letsingers' efforts have paid off, and they have been lauded for all that they have done. Working with the Alabama District Attorneys Association, they helped pass legislation that specifies exactly what constitutes an illegal drug. The law sets fines for those in possession of the drugs and imposes tough penalties for anyone who manufactures and sells them. The legislation, called Landon's Law in their son's memory, took effect in May 2014. "Everything our family has done," says Chris Letsinger, "from getting the new law established to setting up a scholarship for soccer players at Muscle Shoals High School in Landon's name, is all about keeping Landon's memory alive, and getting justice for him."[88]

Building Awareness Among Medical Providers

When people think about action that must be taken to stop the proliferation of synthetic drugs, educating doctors may not come to mind. Yet everyone who works in a health care capacity needs to fully understand what they are dealing with, especially those in emergency medicine. "Education and public awareness efforts must go beyond parents and young adults," says NAAG, "and extend to first responders and emergency room personnel, who must be able to identify the symptoms of synthetic drug use in order to provide appropriate and effective care."[89]

According to data compiled by the National Council on Alcoholism and Drug Dependence, when the bath salts crisis first emerged in the United States only about half of emergency room doctors had even heard of synthetic drugs. Even doctors who knew of the drugs were not always clear about how patients should be treated. Says NAAG: "Emergency room and urgent care clinicians should be educated on the signs and symptoms of intoxication and be urged to reach out to toxicologists, poison control centers and other drug experts whenever necessary. Doctors who are unfamiliar with synthetic drugs and their effects run the risk of misdiagnosis."[90]

The viewpoint that many emergency physicians are not well informed about synthetic drugs was reinforced during a study published in September 2013. It was led by Patrick M. Lank, an emergency medicine physician at Northwestern University's Feinberg School of Medicine in Chicago, Illinois. The research involved an anonymous survey of seventy-three resident and attending physicians at a large urban emergency room. The goal of the study was to evaluate the doctors' familiarity with the terms *Spice* or *K2*, and to assess their knowledge of synthetic cannabinoids.

One finding was that fewer than half of the respondents were familiar with Spice and K2 and did not associate the terms with synthetic cannabinoids. What knowledge the doctors did possess about the drugs most often came from nonmedical sources, such as lay publications and the Internet. Among those with previous knowledge of synthetic cannabinoids, 25 percent were not aware that the substances were synthetic drugs, and 17 percent did not know they were chemically similar to marijuana. Just four of the seventy-three physicians had ever discussed synthetic drugs with a patient, and only three had taken care of a patient who had used Spice or K2.

All in all, Lank and his colleagues found the study quite revealing. Once all the responses were tabulated, they could see that emergency physicians were seriously lacking in knowledge about synthetic cannabinoids. One particular finding was that 80 percent of the participating doctors reported feeling unprepared to care for patients in the emergency room who had used synthetic cannabinoids. In the September 2013 report of the study, the authors write, "This study brings to light the problems physicians face when treating patients who are using new drugs of abuse. Specifically, it became clear that there is an inherent difficulty in treating patients using a new drug of abuse because of a lack of available medical literature on the substance. . . . More education is needed among [emergency physicians] of all ages and levels of training on synthetic cannabinoids."[91]

One important step toward expanding knowledge of synthetic drugs among medical providers is training paramedics. These are

> "Doctors who are unfamiliar with synthetic drugs and their effects run the risk of misdiagnosis."[90]
>
> — National Association of Attorneys General.

One Special Dog

On November 3, 2014, an eager, energetic springer spaniel hopped out of a car in Douglas County, Georgia, and trotted over to a crowd of people who were waiting for him. The dog's name is Dakota: officially, K-9 Officer Dakota. He was born in the Netherlands and imported to the United States, where he was specially trained at a facility in Sharpsville, Pennsylvania. K-9 Officer Dakota is two years old and a highly specialized drug-sniffing dog. Not only can he sniff out narcotics like marijuana, heroin, methamphetamine, and cocaine, he is also trained to detect synthetic cannabis. K-9 Officer Dakota works alongside five other dogs that are part of the Douglas County sheriff's office K-9 team.

K-9 Officer Dakota's official responsibility is working with the county's middle schools and high schools in Douglas County. Along with his handler, Lieutenant John Jewell, Dakota helps educate students about the dangers of drug use, as well as performs drug detection duties.

called *first responders* for a reason: When someone calls 911 because of a medical emergency, paramedics are often the first to arrive and provide care for the person in trouble. Thus, they need to be trained in all kinds of emergencies, including those that arise from reactions to synthetic drugs.

In May 2015 an ambulance service in Florence, Alabama, hired an instructor to teach two one-hour courses on synthetic drugs to a group of paramedics. The sessions covered the basic signs to look for in order to determine if someone has taken synthetic drugs. These signs include violent, delusional behavior or other symptoms that are unlike those of a traditional drug overdose. The paramedics were also taught how to treat and handle overdose victims.

According to Blake Hargett, operations manager of the ambulance service, this training was timely because synthetic drug cases are happening more often. "It's out on the streets," he says. "It's real. And the public needs to know about it."[92]

Educating and Warning Retailers

One of the greatest hindrances to law enforcement's ability to fight synthetic drugs is that the drugs are still often sold openly in tobacco shops, head shops, gas stations, and convenience stores. Those who are involved in the fight against synthetic drugs emphasize that retailers must be made aware of the dangerous and often illegal nature of these substances. This could, of course, reduce the number of drugs that are out among the public. But it could also contribute to law enforcement's ability to prosecute a retailer for selling the drugs, as NAAG explains: "Proof that a retailer was warned and continued to sell the substances is also helpful for a prosecutor working to establish intent at that retailer's trial." The group goes on to say that in recent years, the states and the federal government have used a number of tactics to put retailers on notice. "Initially, retailers were not very responsive," says NAAG. "As the problems associated with these substances have become worse, retail associations have become more cooperative."[93]

At a September 2013 hearing titled "Dangerous Synthetic Drugs," the DEA's Joseph T. Rannazzisi was one of the officials who testified. Rannazazisi shared an unfortunate reality: that despite progress that has been made to stop retailers from selling synthetic drugs, the drugs continued to be sold in stores throughout the United States. In an effort to put an even bigger dent in this practice the DEA sent a letter in June 2013 to each of the top one hundred retail convenience store and gas station chain corporations in the United States. They were informed of the alarming trend of the sale and abuse of synthetic designer drugs that were disingenuously being sold as over-the-counter household items such as bath salts, incense, or jewelry cleaner. As Rannazzisi explains: "The letter discussed why they are marketed and sold at retail, how they

are abused and the health consequences and the dangers associated with the abuse of these substances. The letter requested that these corporations take steps to protect the public by preventing these substances from being sold at their business locations."[94]

Rannazzisi goes on to say that the corporations were invited to attend a seminar in Arlington, Virginia, on August 8, 2013, titled "The Dangers of Designer Synthetic Drugs." The seminar was an in-depth presentation about the synthetic drug problem in the United States. Participants were educated about the dangers and consequences of selling synthetic drugs, and they were also taught how to identify the products. "Only four corporations attended the seminar," says Rannazzisi. "However, the four companies (Shell Oil, Marathon Petroleum, Citgo, and TA-Petro) have a large number of retail outlets throughout the United States and one corporation that has a network of over 14,000 branded stations in the United States indicated they were taking proactive

In 2015 attorneys general in forty-three states sent a letter to executives of nine oil companies urging them to stop sales of synthetic drugs at their gas stations and convenience stores. The letter expressed grave concern about availability of the drugs in these types of locations.

A Controversial Solution

Virtually everyone, from health officials to law enforcement, substance abuse experts, educators, and parents, agrees that something must be done to address the problem of synthetic drugs. What that "something" is, however, is an issue of much debate. Tougher laws, community awareness programs, education programs for kids, and partnerships with retailers are just a few of the strategies that have been implemented to fight the synthetic drug problem in the United States. One solution that is supported by a number of individuals is the legalization of marijuana. Advocates say that if marijuana were legal, the market for synthetic cannabis, which is the most widely used of all synthetic drugs, could potentially disappear. John W. Huffman, the scientist who originally created synthetic cannabinoids for research purposes, is one of marijuana legalization's staunchest supporters, as he explains:

> I do believe that if marijuana had been legal, the synthetic material never would have become the problem that it is today. No one ever died from an overdose of marijuana, but there have been a number of deaths caused by the use of synthetic marijuana. I support the legalization of marijuana for the same reason. It is the only approach that I believe would work.

John W. Huffman, e-mail interview with author, May 21, 2015.

measures in demanding that if these products are being sold in their stores, they are taken off of the shelves immediately."[95]

More recently, in February 2015 forty-three attorneys general sent a letter to the chief executives of nine oil companies: British Petroleum (BP), Chevron, Citgo Petroleum, Exxon Mobil, Marathon Petroleum, Phillips 66, Shell Oil, Sunoco, and Valero Energy. The letter requested that the companies make it a priority to stop synthetic drugs from being sold at their gas stations and convenience stores. The attorneys general stated that they were writing the letter "to express our deep concerns over the problem of gas stations and convenience stores operating under the brand names of your companies and selling synthetic drugs that are illegal and extremely dangerous. Given the significant danger synthetic drugs present to users, especially our young people, we are extremely troubled that these drugs have been readily available in well-known retail locations."[96]

At the end of the letter was a specific request for the CEOs of the oil companies:

> We ask that you work with us in our efforts to eliminate synthetic drugs from retail locations. Young people should not die or be seriously injured from using products bought at gas stations or convenience stores. While we acknowledge that the sale of synthetic drugs at retail locations is only one aspect of an ongoing problem, we do know it has greatly contributed to the growth of the problem.[97]

The attorneys general who signed the letter hope that forming partnerships with the major oil companies will be one more way of attempting to keep synthetic drugs out of the public's hands—and one more way to keep kids from dying.

Future Uncertainties

Even though synthetic drugs have existed in the United States for less than a decade, they have wreaked havoc on the country. People who never heard of the drugs find out that their kids have used them and sometimes died from them. Health officials and many in law enforcement acknowledge the importance of tough legislation—but it is becoming clear that laws alone are not enough. Young people need to be educated about the risks of the drugs, as do parents, educators, police officers, paramedics, and even physicians who may be able to easily spot a heroin addict but have no idea what to look for in a synthetic drug user. These and other preventive measures will hopefully help to curb the growth of dangerous synthetic drugs.

Facts

- According to the group DoSomething.org, teens who consistently learn about the risks of drugs from their parents are up to 50 percent less likely to use drugs than those who do not.

- After the United Kingdom listed synthetic cannabinoids as controlled substances, the ban spurred development of new synthetic cannabinoid products.

- In March 2013 fifty-five countries voted to create an international early warning system, which enables countries to share data quickly when investigators first hear of new synthetic drug compounds.

- Despite New York's efforts to control synthetic drug abuse, the New York City Department of Health and Mental Hygiene reported that emergency room visits related to synthetic cannabis were up 220 percent in the first half of 2014.

- After the Synthetic Drug Abuse Prevention Act took effect in 2012, there was a sharp decline in synthetic drug use; but according to American Association of Poison Control Center data, emergency calls to poison centers in 2014 far outpaced those from 2013.

Source Notes

Introduction: Chasing a Deadly High

1. Quoted in Ryan Korsgard, "Texas Senate Aims to Change Laws Involving Synthetic Drugs," Click2Houston, March 10, 2015. www.click2houston.com.

2. Drug Enforcement Administration, *2015 International Narcotics Control Strategy Report*, March 18, 2015. www.state.gov.

3. Quoted in Deborah Brauser, "New Deadly Class of Synthetic Hallucinogens Mimics LSD," Medscape, December 10, 2014. www.medscape.com.

4. National Institute on Drug Abuse, "Emerging Trends," May 2015. www.drugabuse.gov.

5. Quoted in Larissa Scott, "Synthetic Drugs Cause Similar Medical Calls," MyPanhandle, May 6, 2015. www.mypanhandle.com.

6. Quoted in Associated Press, "Synthetic Marijuana-Related Hospitalizations Skyrocket in US," *Guardian* (Manchester), May 8, 2015. www.theguardian.com.

7. Drug Enforcement Administration, *2015 National Drug Threat Assessment Summary*, February 2, 2015. www.dea.gov.

8. Quoted in Dane Schiller, "Houston Gains Key Role in Synthetic Marijuana," *Houston Chronicle*, November 30, 2013. www.houstonchronicle.com.

Chapter One: What Are the Origins of the Synthetic Drug Problem?

9. Mark Ryan, interview with author, May 19, 2015.

10. Ryan, interview with author.

11. Ryan, interview with author.

12. Ryan, interview with author.

13. Ryan, interview with author.

14. Ryan, interview with author.

15. Quoted in Jenny Marder, "The Drug That Never Lets Go," *PBS NewsHour*, September 20, 2012. www.pbs.org.

16. Quoted in Marcy Mason, "Lethal Highs," *Frontline Magazine*, Fall 2013. www.cbp.gov.

17. Quoted in Mason, "Lethal Highs."

18. Mason, "Lethal Highs."

19. National Institute on Drug Abuse, "Drugs and the Brain," July 2014. www.drugabuse.gov.

20. John W. Huffman, e-mail interview with author, May 21, 2015.

21. Huffman, e-mail interview with author.

22. Huffman, e-mail interview with author.

23. Quoted in Marder, "The Drug That Never Lets Go."

24. Marder, "The Drug That Never Lets Go."

25. Quoted in Marder, "The Drug That Never Lets Go."

26. Quoted in Mason, "Lethal Highs."

Chapter Two: Why Are Young People Drawn to Synthetic Drugs?

27. Donna M. Lisi, "Patients May Be Using Synthetic Cannabinoids More than You Think," *JEMS* (*Journal of Emergency Medical Services*), May 2015. www.jems.com.

28. Quoted in Fox News, "FOX 5 Investigates: DC Leaders, Police Pushing to Get Synthetic Marijuana off the Streets," May 15, 2013. www.myfoxdc.com.

29. Raychelle Cassada Lohmann, "Lethally High: Teenagers and Synthetic Drugs," Rehabs.com Pro Talk, January 6, 2015. www.rehabs.com.

30. Greg Thrash, in Chris Sedechi, "Synthetic Drugs Sold Using Sly, Deceptive Marketing," video, KXAN, May 21, 2014. http://kxan.com.

31. John Bedolla, in Sedechi, "Synthetic Drugs Sold Using Sly, Deceptive Marketing," video.

32. Lohmann, "Lethally High."

33. Quoted in Teresa Stepzinski, "Despite Playful Packaging Designed to Attract Teens, Synthetic Drugs Contain Real Danger," *Florida Times-Union*, October 3, 2014. http://jacksonville.com.

34. Ryan, interview with author.

35. Ryan, interview with author.

36. Lloyd D. Johnston et al., "Monitoring the Future: 2014 Overview," February 2015. http://monitoringthefuture.org.

37. Quoted in Liam Burke, "A Mother's Message: Synthetic Drugs Designed to Pass High School Drug Tests," *Standard Examiner* (Ogden, UT), December 7, 2014. www.standard.net.

38. American Academy of Child and Adolescent Psychiatry, "The Teen Brain: Behavior, Problem Solving, and Decision Making," *Facts for Families*, December 2011. www.aacap.org.

39. National Institute of Mental Health, "The Teen Brain: Still Under Construction," 2011. www.nimh.nih.gov.

40. National Institute of Mental Health, "The Teen Brain: Still Under Construction."

41. Quoted in NPR, "Why Teens Are Impulsive, Addiction-Prone and Should Protect Their Brains," January 28, 2015. www.npr.org.

42. Joseph J. Palamar and Patricia Acosta, "Synthetic Cannabinoid Use in a Nationally Representative Sample of US High School Seniors," *Drug and Alcohol Dependence*, April 2015, p. 194.

43. Quoted in New York University, news release, "NYU Study Identifies Teens At-Risk for Synthetic Marijuana Use," February 28, 2015. www.nyu.edu.

44. Palamar and Acosta, "Synthetic Cannabinoid Use in a Nationally Representative Sample of US High School Seniors," p. 198.

Chapter Three: What Are the Dangers of Synthetic Drug Use?

45. Quoted in Tonya Alanez and Emily Miller, "Rescue of Man Impaled on Security Gate a Risky Undertaking," *South Florida Sun-Sentinel*, March 25, 2015. www.sun-sentinel.com.

46. Quoted in Dennis Thompson, "New Synthetic Drug 'Flakka' Triggers Crazed Behaviors," *Merck Manual*, April 16, 2015. www.merckmanuals.com.

47. Quoted in Tonya Alanez, "Flakka: Rampant Designer Drug Dubbed '$5 Insanity,'" *South Florida Sun-Sentinel*, April 5, 2015. www.sun-sentinel.com.

48. Quoted in Curt Anderson, "Naked, 'Superhuman' and Convinced You're Being Followed? That's Flakka," *Toronto Star*, April 30, 2015. www.thestar.com.

49. Quoted in Ted Scouten, "Exclusive: Man Fueled by 'Flakka' Tries to Kick in Door at Police Headquarters," CBS Miami, March 11, 2015. http://miami.cbslocal.com.

50. Quoted in Alanez and Miller, "Rescue of Man Impaled on Security Gate a Risky Undertaking."

51. Quoted in Dane Schiller, "Officials Say 'Fake Pot' Sparks Dramatic Climb in Overdoses," *Houston Chronicle*, January 18, 2015. www.houstonchronicle.com.

52. Quoted in Schiller, "Officials Say 'Fake Pot' Sparks Dramatic Climb in Overdoses."

53. Huffman, e-mail interview with author.

54. Quoted in Bruce Hensel and Matthew Glasser, "Dangerous Designer Drugs on the Rise with Teens," NBC Los Angeles, February 6, 2015. www.nbclosangeles.com.

55. Quoted in Hensel and Glasser, "Dangerous Designer Drugs on the Rise with Teens."

56. Quoted in Hensel and Glasser, "Dangerous Designer Drugs on the Rise with Teens."

57. Quoted in Mason, "Lethal Highs."

58. Quoted in Prue Salasky, "Teen Spice User: 'It's the New Crack,'" *Daily Press* (Newport News, VA), May 18, 2014. http://articles.dailypress.com.

59. Quoted in Salasky, "Teen Spice User: 'It's the New Crack.'"

60. Quoted in Petrina J. Johnson, "Cypress Teen Recovering Two Years After Smoking Synthetic Marijuana," *Cypress Creek Mirror*, February 2015. http://m.yourhoustonnews.com.

61. Ryan, interview with author.

62. Quoted in Jim Anderson and Kevin Giles, "For Victims, Synthetic Drugs Are Deadly Game of 'Russian Roulette,'" *Duluth (MN) News Tribune*, May 30, 2014. www.duluthnewstribune.com.

Chapter Four: What Legal Challenges Are Associated with Synthetic Drugs?

63. Alan Schwarz, "Arrest Underscores China's Role in the Making and Spread of a Lethal Drug," *New York Times*, May 28, 2015. www.nytimes.com.

64. US Drug Enforcement Administration news release, "Top China-Based Global Designer Drug Trafficker Arrested in U.S.," May 28, 2015. www.dea.gov.

65. Quoted in Schwarz, "Arrest Underscores China's Role in the Making and Spread of a Lethal Drug."

66. US Drug Enforcement Administration news release, "Top China-Based Global Designer Drug Trafficker Arrested in U.S."

67. Quoted in Alan Schwarz, "Surge in Hospital Visits Linked to a Drug Called Spice Alarms Health Officials," *New York Times*, April 24, 2015. www.nytimes.com.

68. National Association of Attorneys General, "Designer Drugs Lead to Designer Legislation," *NAAGazette*, February 28, 2014. www.naag.org.

69. Quoted in Joel Rose, "Fake Pot Is a Real Problem for Regulators," NPR, July 12, 2012. www.npr.org.

70. John Parr, "The Synthetic Drug Abuse Prevention Act: There's Still Heavy Lifting to Do Hurdles in Prosecuting Synthetic Drug Cases," *Ohio State Journal of Criminal Law*, November 20, 2012. http://moritzlaw.osu.edu.

71. National Association of Attorneys General, "Designer Drugs Lead to Designer Legislation."

72. Quoted in Olga Khazan, "Synthetic Drugs Are Multiplying Too Fast for Regulators to Outlaw Them," *Atlantic*, June 27, 2013. www.theatlantic.com.

73. Ryan, interview with author.

74. National Conference on State Legislatures, "Synthetic Drug Threats," January 13, 2015. www.ncsl.org.

75. National Conference on State Legislatures, "Synthetic Drug Threats."

76. Quoted in Mason, "Lethal Highs."

77. Quoted in Brian Haas, "Store Owners Admit to Selling Synthetic Pot," *Tennessean*, February 7, 2014. www.tennessean.com.

78. Jason Nevel, "State Ban Curbs Synthetic Drug Use," *State Journal-Register* (Springfield, IL), June 6, 2013. www.sj-r.com.

79. Quoted in X95, "State Senate Approves McCarter Measure Targeting Synthetic Drugs," April 23, 2015. www.x95radio.com.

80. Quoted in Mason, "Lethal Highs."

Chapter Five: What Can Be Done About Synthetic Drug Abuse?

81. Richard M. Nixon, in John T. Woolley and Gerhard Peters, "Statement About the Drug Abuse Office and Treatment Act of 1972," The American Presidency Project. www.presidency.ucsb.edu.

82. National Association of Attorneys General, "Education and Prevention Initiatives as Necessary Tools to Combat Synthetic Drug Abuse," May 29, 2014. www.naag.org.

83. National Association of Attorneys General, "Education and Prevention Initiatives as Necessary Tools to Combat Synthetic Drug Abuse."

84. National Association of Attorneys General, "Education and Prevention Initiatives as Necessary Tools to Combat Synthetic Drug Abuse."

85. Keith Bjerk and Debbie Bjerk, "Mourning Family: Why Synthetic Drugs Are Your Problem Too," CNN, December 1, 2014. www.cnn.com.

86. Bjerk and Bjerk, "Mourning Family."

87. Quoted in Marie Waxel, "A Shoals Mother Whose Son Died from Spice Wants to Save Others," WorldNow, May 16, 2015. http://raycomnbc.worldnow.com.

88. Quoted in Tom Smith, "Arrest Made in Fatal Overdose," *TimesDaily* (Florence, AL), October 7, 2014. www.timesdaily .com.

89. National Association of Attorneys General, "Education and Prevention Initiatives as Necessary Tools to Combat Synthetic Drug Abuse."

90. National Association of Attorneys General, "Education and Prevention Initiatives as Necessary Tools to Combat Synthetic Drug Abuse."

91. Patrick M. Lank, Elizabeth Pines, and Mark B. Mycyk, "Emergency Physicians' Knowledge of Cannabinoid Designer Drugs," *Western Journal of Emergency Medicine*, September 2013. www.ncbi.nlm.nih.gov.

92. Quoted in Catherine Awasthi, "Paramedics Learn to Respond to & Treat Synthetic Drug Overdoses," WHNT, May 20, 2015. http://whnt.com.

93. National Association of Attorneys General, "Education and Prevention Initiatives as Necessary Tools to Combat Synthetic Drug Abuse."

94. Joseph T. Rannazzisi, "Statement Before the Caucus on International Narcotics Control, United States Senate, for a Hearing Entitled 'Dangerous Synthetic Drugs,'" September 25, 2013. www.dea.gov.

95. Rannazzisi, "Statement Before the Caucus on International Narcotics Control, United States Senate, for a Hearing Entitled 'Dangerous Synthetic Drugs.'"

96. National Association of Attorneys General, letter to major oil companies, February 10, 2015. www.ncdoj.gov.

97. National Association of Attorneys General, letter to major oil companies.

Related Organizations and Websites

American Association of Poison Control Centers (AAPCC)
515 King St., Suite 510
Alexandria, VA 22314
phone: (703) 894-1858
e-mail: info@aapcc.org • website: www.aapcc.org

The AAPCC is the parent organization for fifty-five poison control centers throughout the United States, and it maintains the country's only comprehensive poisoning surveillance database. Its website offers a large collection of data and statistics about synthetic drugs.

Community Anti-Drug Coalitions of America (CADCA)
625 Slaters Ln., Suite 300
Alexandria, VA 22314
phone: (800) 542-2322 • fax: (703) 706-0565
e-mail: info@cadca.org • website: www.cadca.org

Representing more than five thousand community coalitions and affiliates, the CADCA seeks to make America's communities safe, healthy, and drug free. Its website offers policy information, news articles, and a search engine that produces numerous publications about synthetic drugs.

Council on Chemical Abuse

601 Penn St., Suite 600
Reading, PA 19601
phone: (610) 376-8669 • fax: (610) 376-8423
website: www.councilonchemicalabuse.org

The Council on Chemical Abuse serves as the coordinating agency for publicly supported programming on drug and alcohol abuse throughout Berks County, Pennsylvania. Numerous articles and fact sheets about synthetic drugs are available through its website.

Drug Enforcement Administration (DEA)

8701 Morrissette Dr.
Springfield, VA 22152
phone: (202) 307-1000
website: www.dea.gov • teen website: www.justthinktwice.com

An agency of the US Department of Justice, the DEA is the United States' leading law enforcement agency for combating the sale and distribution of narcotics and other illegal drugs. Its website links to a separate teen site that provides a wealth of information about drugs, including synthetic drugs.

Drug Free America Foundation

5999 Central Ave., Suite 301
Saint Petersburg, FL 33710
phone: (727) 828-0211 • fax: (727) 828-0212
e-mail: webmaster@dfaf.org • website: www.dfaf.org

The Drug Free America Foundation is a drug prevention and policy organization. Its website has a special section titled "Synthetic/Designer Drugs," as well as a search engine that produces numerous articles about synthetic drugs.

Drug Policy Alliance

131 West 33rd St., 15th Floor
New York, NY 10001
phone: (212) 613-8020 • fax: (212) 613-8021
e-mail: nyc@drugpolicy.org • website: www.drugpolicy.org

The Drug Policy Alliance promotes alternatives to current drug policy that are grounded in science, compassion, health, and human rights. Its website features drug facts, statistics, information about drug laws, and a search engine that produces a number of articles about synthetic drugs.

Foundation for a Drug-Free World

1626 N. Wilcox Ave., Suite 1297
Los Angeles, CA 90028
phone: (818) 952-5260; toll-free: (888) 668-6378
e-mail: info@drugfreeworld.org • website: www.drugfreeworld.org

Foundation for a Drug-Free World provides factual information about drugs to youth and adults to help them make informed decisions and live drug free. A wealth of information is available on the interactive website, including articles specifically related to synthetic drug abuse.

National Institute on Drug Abuse (NIDA)

National Institutes of Health
6001 Executive Blvd., Room 5213
Bethesda, MD 20892-9561
phone: (301) 443-1124
e-mail: information@nida.nih.gov • website: www.drugabuse.gov

NIDA supports research efforts that improve drug abuse prevention, treatment, and policy. The website links to a separate "NIDA for Teens" site, which is designed especially for young people and provides a wealth of information about drugs, including synthetic drugs.

Office of National Drug Control Policy

750 Seventeenth St. NW
Washington, DC 20503
phone: (800) 666-3332 • fax: (202) 395-6708
e-mail: ondcp@ncjrs.org • website: www.whitehouse.gov/ondcp

A component of the executive office of the president, the Office of National Drug Control Policy is responsible for directing the federal government's antidrug programs. A wide variety of publications about synthetic drugs can be accessed through the site's search engine.

Partnership for Drug-Free Kids (formerly Partnership at DrugFree.org)
352 Park Ave. South, 9th Floor
New York, NY 10010
phone: (212) 922-1560 • fax: (212) 922-1570
website: www.drugfree.org

The Partnership for Drug-Free Kids is dedicated to helping parents and families solve the problem of teenage substance abuse. Informative publications and current articles about synthetic drugs are accessible through its website.

Substance Abuse and Mental Health Services Administration (SAMHSA)
1 Choke Cherry Rd.
Rockville, MD 20857
phone: (877) 726-4727 • fax: (240) 221-4292
e-mail: samhsainfo@samhsa.hhs.gov • website: www.samhsa.gov

SAMHSA's mission is to reduce the impact of substance abuse and mental illness on America's communities. The site offers numerous articles, fact sheets, and other types of publications about synthetic drugs.

To the Maximus Foundation
1120 Grenada Dr.
Aurora, IL 60506
phone: (630) 892-3629
e-mail: info@2themax.org • website: http://2themax.org

Created in memory of a teen who died after using synthetic marijuana, To the Maximus Foundation is committed to education and awareness of the dangers of synthetic drugs. Its website offers news releases, fact sheets, testimonials, links to other resources, and a blog.

Additional Reading

Books

William Dudley, *Synthetic Drug Addiction*. San Diego: ReferencePoint, 2015.

Hazelden Foundation, *Get Smart About Synthetic Drugs*. Center City, MN: Hazelden, 2013.

Peggy J. Parks, *Bath Salts and Other Synthetic Drugs*. San Diego: ReferencePoint, 2014.

Mary E. Williams, ed., *Synthetic Drugs*. Detroit, MI: Greenhaven, 2014.

Periodicals

Lydia Denworth, "Scary Spice," *Choices/Current Health*, April 2014.

David diSalvo, "The Backstory You Really Need to Know About Flakka and Other Synthetic Drugs," *Forbes*, April 15, 2015.

Economist, "New Highs: Recreational Drug Use," May 24, 2014.

Eliza Gray, "The Rise of Fake Pot," *Time*, April 10, 2014.

Alan Schwarz, "Potent 'Spice' Drug Fuels Rise in Visits to Emergency Rooms," *New York Times*, April 24, 2015.

Dennis Thompson, "New Synthetic Drug 'Flakka' Triggers Crazed Behaviors," *Consumer Health News*, April 16, 2015.

Internet Sources

Drew Griffin and Nelli Black, "Deadly High: How Synthetic Drugs Are Killing Kids," CNN, December 2, 2014. www.cnn .com/2014/12/01/us/synthetic-drugs-investigation.

Susan Donaldson James, "Flakka: New Synthetic Drug Is More Potent than Predecessors," NBC News, April 15, 2015. www .nbcnews.com/health/health-news/flakka-attack-new-synth etic-drug-joins-list-spanning-lsd-molly-n341506.

Marcy Mason, US Customs and Border Protection, "Lethal Highs," *Frontline Magazine*, Fall 2013. www.cbp.gov/sites/de fault/files/documents/Lethal_Highs_frontline_fall2013-2 .pdf.

National Institute on Drug Abuse, "Emerging Trends," May 2015. www.drugabuse.gov/drugs-abuse/emerging-trends.

Index

Picture Credits

AP Images: 19, 29, 49

© Tony Arruza/Corbis: 73

Broward Sheriff's Office/AP Images: 42

Depositphotos: 68

Steve Gschmeissner/Science Source: 45

© Scott Houston/Sygma/Corbis: 60

© Jay Laprete/Reuters/Corbis: 23

© Yang Liu/Corbis: 55

Mark M. Miller/Science Source: 36

© Andy Mills/Star Ledger/Corbis: 15

© Patrick Pleul/dpa/Corbis: 10

© Stringer/Mexico/Reuters/Corbis: 32

About the Author

Peggy J. Parks holds a bachelor of science degree from Aquinas College in Grand Rapids, Michigan, where she graduated magna cum laude. An author who has written dozens of educational books on a wide variety of topics for children and young adults, Parks lives in Muskegon, Michigan, a town that she says inspires her writing because of its location on the shores of Lake Michigan.